Barfani Baba

To Amarnath, Happily

Barfani Baba

To Amarnath, Happily

ABHA VATSA

Vitasta
Let Knowledge Spread

Times Group Books

Published by Renu Kaul Verma for
Vitasta Publishing Pvt Ltd
2/15, Ansari Road, Daryaganj,
New Delhi - 110 002
info@vitastapublishing.com

ISBN 978-93-80828-30-5

Layout Design by Vitasta Publishing Pvt Ltd
Cover Design by Aditya Rai
Printed by Vikas Computer and Printers, New Delhi
Photo Credits: Abha Vatsa, Dr Pradeep Agarwal

Marketed and Distributed exclusively in India & Sub-Continent by:

Times Group Books

Times Group Books
(A division of Bennett, Coleman and Company Limited)
Times Annexe, Express Building
9-10 Bahadur Shah Zafar Marg, New Delhi-110 002

For Mum and Dad
and my
Maternal Grandmother (Naniji)

Preface

As I start typing the manuscript of my first ever book, a Spiritual Travelogue, I can't help but wonder at the mysteries that time holds in its folds. A blogger for two years, I never planned to take up writing, even though I loved literature in spite of being primarily a science student.

Ever since I took up blogging, the writing scene strengthened from one post to the next and somewhere at the back of my mind was the prospect of writing a book and getting it published.

Did I plan a Spiritual Travelogue? No. But the seeds were already planted. By the *sanskaars* given to me by my parents, especially my father, who has a philosophical bent of mind. And when the timing was right, those seeds sprouted in the form of a desire to visit Amarnath and chronicle my experiences in the form of a book.

I grew up in a middle class Hindu family which follow the Sanatam Dharma way of life. So the concept of God, prayers, rituals, mythology, fasting, *satsang* was part of my growing up years in Allahabad.

I distinctly remember one incident from childhood. One day my father narrated to me the story of Shravan Kumar. Children love stories and I listened to him in rapt attention.

The story went like this:

Shravan Kumar belonged to the time when King Dashratha ruled Ayodhya. He was born to a Vaishanava Brahmin father Shantnav and a Vaishnav Shudra mother Gyanvati.

One day his parents told him that they had become quite aged. They, therefore, wanted him to take them to the forty places of pilgrimage. It is a typical Hindu belief that a pilgrimage to the various shrines and holy places undertaken in old age purifies the soul.

In those days, transportation was scarce and Shravan Kumar could not afford it. He, therefore, decided to place his parents in two baskets and carry the baskets on his shoulder to the various places of pilgrimage. He took a strong bamboo stick, at its two ends he tied the two baskets with strong ropes, and placed his father in one of the basket and his mother in the other. Carrying on his shoulder this bamboo stick with a basket at each end, Shravan started on the pilgrimage.

According to the story in Ramayana, while hunting in the forest of Ayodhya, King Dashratha heard a sound near a lake and unleashed an arrow, hoping to hit an animal.When he crossed the lake to collect his kill, he found that his arrow had struck a boy who was bleeding.

At this point, Dad sung a couplet:

Zaalim maine tera kya bigada
Teer tune jo seene main mara

As I heard these words,tears rolled down my eyes. I was always a sensitive child.

The story continued:

The boy, Shravan Kumar, told Dashratha that he had come to the lake to collect water for his sick and aged parents, who were both blind and who he had been carrying on a sling. He requested the King to take water to his parents. After telling his tale, Shravan succumbed to his wounds and when the King took water for his parents and told them of his tragic mistake, they were unable to bear the shock.

They cursed the King that he, too, would meet his death caused by the sorrow of separation from his son just as what had happened to them. Shortly afterwards, both the parents passed away.

This was my first awareness of a *teerath* or *pilgrimage*.

The second came from the memory of my Nani, my maternal grandmother.

My Nani became a widow before my mother was married. I have memories of her as a gutsy strong woman who lived her life on her own terms, her head held high.

I have fond memories of spending summer holidays in Phagwara where she lived. The fact that I was born in Phagwara in her home and not in a hospital is the reason I have special attachment to that home, her and Phagwara.

Like any devout Hindu, she had a Guru, a female one. This Guru decided to take all her female devotees on a 40 city pilgrimage via train. It was when she touched Allahabad and visited our home during the pilgrimage that I had the second awareness of relevance of a pilgrimage.

Hence, it is little wonder that I am dedicating this book to both her and my parents.

Right behind my home, in my neighborhood, is a Shiv Shakti temple, which also doubles as a *satsang* venue and a meeting place for neighbours.

For several years, I would see a banner of Amarnath Yatra displayed on the front gate of the temple. This year, I had a strong urge to visit Amarnath. This is how this book happened.

Om Namah Shivay

It is said that *saawan ke andhe ko sab kuch hara hi hara dikhayi deta hai.* Once I had made up my mind to go to Amarnath, my every waking thought was of the *Yatra*, and having *darshan* of the Barfani Baba, the ice Shivling at the Holy Cave.

I did not know then that my response to the call of the Barfani Baba would begin at an ancient Shiv temple, right here in Faridabad's old bustling market place. The Barfani Baba was still with my wish tree when, one day, I went to the market for routine purchases and spotted a hoarding on the Amarnath Yatra.

The fervour around the annual pilgrimage was infectious. I had heard of a gentleman in my neighbourhood by the name of P L Arora, who was not only a member of the temple governing body but a devout Shiv *bhakt*. I had also heard that he had been going to Amarnath regularly for more than a decade. I knew he was just the right person to ask for guidance. So I went to his house, my first ever visit to his place.

'Uncle' knew me by face as he had visited our home whenever I had organized a *prabhaat pheri*, an early morning neighbourhood procession and singing, in the month of *Karthik*. He was extremely kind, encouraging and helpful. On the very first day, he gave me the two registration forms that needed to be filled to get civic permission to go on this Yatra in the border state of Jammu and Kashmir. He also gave me a small pamphlet with the route of the Yatra. I knew then that my journey to Amarnath had already begun.

He also gave me a poster by tour operators, which had a route of our journey from Faridabad to Amarnath and back to Faridabad, along with a list of important items to carry: Woolens, raincoat, torch, medicines, Boroplus ointment, dry fruits, sports shoes with laces, glucose etc.

It was here that I first heard of places like Chandanwari, Sheshnag, Sangam, Panchtarni etc.

Before the journey began I went to Uncle's

house a couple of times and to my surprise, he too dropped in a few times to guide me and help me prepare for the Yatra.

I had already booked my seats in the bus and paid part of the fare to Uncle. Five days before the Yatra was to commence, I decided to go to the tour operator's office personally, to pay the balance.

As I crossed the busy marketplace, I saw an erected gate, with a welcome message for Shiv Shankar, and many more hoardings of *bhandaras* on the route to Amarnath, displayed in the market. As the road was congested with parked vehicles, I decided to visit the market again the next morning, to take a few photographs.

The next morning, four days before the Yatra, I drove to the market at 5.30 to capture the ambience.

So engrossed was I in taking photographs that I did not realize that the walls displaying the hoardings belonged to a *pracheen Shivlaya*, an old Shiv temple. I quickly went back to the car to leave the camera and tip-toed into the temple. The welcome entrance gate now made sense.

This *pracheen Shivlaya* is a huge sprawling temple with two ancient trees preserved within the premises. I walked towards the deity and squatted on the floor before it. A group of women were seated on the floor around the temple, offering *abhishek* and reciting *mantras*.

A few minutes later, a woman came up to me

and enquired, 'Do you want to offer water to the Shivling?'

'Yes!' I smiled back at her.

As I extended my hand for the copper *lota* she held, she said, 'Wait. I'l get water for you.'

She was soon back with the pot full of water and handed it to me. I poured the water over Shiv *parivar* and the Shivling, and the next instant another woman handed me marigold flowers. I offered these and yet another woman handed me Bel *patta*. Then another *chandan*. Then rice grains, then sugar. And finally *dhoop*.

I closed my eyes and sat down, listening to the shlokas of Lord Shiv the women were reciting.

I explored the entire temple and then walked out. I crossed the road to get a full view of the temple front. And just then, a gentleman who ran a grocery shop right opposite to the temple stopped me and enquired, 'Where are you from?'

I realized he had seen me take pictures. By now I was used to people's curiosity whenever I clicked photographs in a busy area for my blog posts.Only, this time, the pictures were for my travelogue on my Amarnath Yatra.

'I am from Faridabad. Am going to Amaranth with the tour and plan to write about my experiences.'

'You will get all the information. We have a *bhandara* there. Give us an opportunity to serve you. Tomorrow the *Shobha Yatra* will start from here.'

'What time?' I enquired.

'4.30', he replied.

So, the next day, promptly at 4.30, I parked myself at the little grocery store opposite the *pracheen Shivlaya*.

The atmosphere in the market was one of festivity. Several vehicles covered with red *chunri* and displaying messages of the Shiv Shankar Mandal, and the *bhandaras* were lined up. Little children pranced about in excitement. A panel of *sevadhars* sat outside the temple to collect donations. One counter was offering cold drinks to the gathering. Another shop was giving food to the devout.

A band of musicians with their instruments and in their colourful uniforms stood in a line.

A truck full of grocery for *bhandaras* was ready to take off for Baltal. And then a man walked by, holding on to a bull dressed as Nandi, Shiv's mascot.

Open vehicles with tableaus of Lord Shiv passed by. Soon a man with a mike started singing Shiv *bhajans*, accompanied by the band musicians. There was a flurry of activity as men in white *kurta-pyjamas* crossed the road, getting ready for the *Shobha Yatra*, which was to march across the town for a distance of over 4 kms. I took some photographs and then returned home.

Our tour was for full nine days. It surely required extensive planning and packing. We had already been given a list of things to be taken by the tour operator, but we had much more to pack for our personal convenience.

So began the process of lists and more lists. It seemed to me the packing process would never end.

Finally, the countdown was over and it was time to set forth on the Yatra.

Hindus believe that the greatest pilgrimage is at the feet of parents, as it is impossible to pay the *rinh* or debt of bringing us into this world and caring for us till we attain adulthood and even beyond, until their last breath.

My elder daughter was accompanying me to the Yatra and before setting off for the Yatra, we went to my parents' house, which is very near to my own home. My mother had prepared for a happy send off. She put *tilak* on my forehead and for my daughter, gave us *shagan*, a goodwish gift, in a closed envelope and two packets of dry fruits, one each for the two of us.

As I hugged her, she chanted *Har Har Mahadev* and Dad joined her. And then we headed to the tour operators' office.

We went to the tour operators office which was near the *pracheen Shivlaya*, at 10 pm. That was our boarding time for the bus that would take us to our destination.

A crowd had gathered there, which was getting bigger by the minute. Six buses would be moving simultaneously to Pahalgam via Punjab. A little investigation revealed that many had come to see off their friends and relatives, and wish them good luck on this difficult pilgrimage.

Two men with *dholkis* around their neck stood by. The tour operator handed us two items which where to remain with us for the entire duration of the Yatra.

One was a cap with the name and telephone number the operator. The other was a specially designed walking stick, with a sharp pointed metal end, to help walk both on the road and in the snow.

The cap was to help identify fellow *yatris* traveling form Faridabad with the tour, as invariably, one would get separated form the group. The common cap would help to identify our group.

We deposited our bags in the back of the bus and just then, the *dholkis* began beating their drums. A few of the men gathered there were garlanded and given red *chunri*, a scarf. There was an atmosphere of gaiety and rejoicing as the *yatris*, or pilgrims, were minutes way from beginning their long-awaited Yatra to Amaranth, followed by a bonus *darshan* of Ma Vaishno Devi on the return journey.

It was 11.30 in the night when, finally, we were told to take our seats as the buses were ready to start. We bid adieu to my husband and younger daughter, who had come to see us off.

Suddenly the chants of *Bam Bam Bhole* filled the

air as excited yatris took their seats and ten minutes later, after praying outside the *pracheen Shivlaya*, we set forth on our dream Yatra.

Barely 15 minutes had passed by when once again there was activity in the bus. A few of our fellow passengers were in high spirits and kept chanting *Har Har Mahadev* and *Bam Bam Bhole*, two of the many Shiv chants which we were to hear throughout our entire Yatra.

I was extremely excited about this journey, and since I was traveling to Amarnath for the very first time, I knew I would need a lot of cooperation from my fellow travellers, sharing my bus. So, I had brought with me *moti choor ke laddoo* as a *prasad*. I handed these to a gentleman whom I instantly knew to be the tour leader. His name was Sunil Khurana (SK). He was a Shiv *bhakt*, who was going to Amaranth for the eleventh consecutive year. It was SK's organizational skills and caring attitude which helped us at every step and made it possible for our Yatra to be a huge success.

Our journey to Pahalgam was after crossing a long list of towns, some heard of, and some unknown. Ambala, Kurali, Ludhiana, Chaklan, Ropar, Solakhiyan, Nawanshahr, Banga, Jalandhar, Kartarpur, Hamira, Subhanpur, Beas, Rayya, Tangra, Amritdar and finally Pathankot.

On 23 June, we stopped by on the highway near Pathankot, adjacent to the Indian Oil petrol pump.

There was a *bhandara* here, our first ever encounter with the numerous Shiv *bhandaras* that dotted all over the entire route to Amaranth and back to Baltal. These *bhandaras* were feeding houses, set up by various charitable organisations and religious sects, who fed the pilgrims going to Amarnath.

It was interesting that at every important juncture, we were greeted with rain. It continued to drizzle throughout our journey. At 11 pm in the night, amid the lightest of showers and *bhajans* of Shiv playing loudly, we had our first taste of *bhandara* food. The sweet dish here was *maal pooye*, which we relished.

Out tour operator and SK, were constantly in touch with authorities at Pahalgam to know the exact details of the Yatra. As we moved back to the bus, we were told that the entry to Pahalgam had not yet been granted due to bad weather, and we might have to go to Vaishno Devi instead and later to Amarnath.

While I have all the devotion for Vaishno Mata, I wanted to conserve all my energy for the difficult Amaranth Yatra. The fact that I had already been to Vaishno Devi and never to Amaranth made my desire for the first visit to Amaranth more strong. So, as we headed towards the Lakhanpur border post and our dinner at the *bhandara*, I constantly kept praying to Lord Shiv to take us to Amarnath first.

Though it was midnight, the Lakhanpur border was abuzz when we reached there. Vendors were selling everything from soft drinks to *poodas* to the famous *ladoos* of Lakhanpur, made out of *daal.* As I looked out of the bus window, I saw that the *ladoos* had sold out. Now the vendor was left only with *chutneys.* Coriander and tamamrind. But he continued to keep the light of his stall on.

The tour operator and SK had been gone for almost two hours while the rest of us sat in the bus and waited. None of the pilgrims could sleep as there was a lot of anxiety regarding whether we would be allowed to move to Pahalgam. At 2 am in the night, SK came inside the bus and said to me, 'Want to eat pooda?'

'No', I shook my head dejectedly.

'Relax', he said.

'We have got permission. We are heading towards Pahalgam.'

A big smile broke out as once again, sounds of *Bam Bam Bhole* filed the air. The bus started on its journey to Pahalgam and finally we dozed off.

Throughout the journey, right from Faridabad to Pahalgam there were songs of Bhole being played on the music system. And in between, we would have performers coming and displaying their skills from other buses.

There was one Shiv *bhakt* who sang songs of Shiv in Punjabi. Then there was another Shiv *bhakt* who enacted a mime on Baba Ram Dev.

Also, throughout the journey to and fro, SK would distribute food items to all yatris, at the same time encouraging everyone to share whatever we had carried for the nine-day Yatra.

There was one particular bhajan which I loved:

Hey Bhole Hey Bhole Shankar,
Padharo, Baithe Chup Ke Kahaan,
Ganga Jaata Mei,
Tumhari Kum Pyaase Yahan

On the morning of the 23rd we were headed towards Pahalgam via Udhampur. At 5.30 am we stopped by at a dhaba called *Sajna da dhaba*.

Here, there is a ladies' toilet and the dhaba owner provides water for ablutions, besides tea at this early hour. A line of buses and SUVs were parked before this dhaba for an early morning break.

We are approximately 26 kms away from Udhampur.

The bus driver told me an interesting story. The place where we had stopped is near village Palan, where there is a temple where villagers believe Vaishno Mata's tiger visits at night.

We passed by Kishanpur town where there is

a Power Grid Corporation of India power plant.

As we reached Udhampur we spotted the Army Public School and the Kendriya Vidyalaya boards on the highway. There is also a Radha Soami Satasng in Udhampur, which is a military cantonment.

We crossed through Kud, a subdivision of the district of Patnitop.

At around 9 am our bus stopped at Chandrakot where there is a power plant of the JP group. Here we were welcomed like special guests as this *bhandara* was set up by the Faridabad Shiv Seva Mandal.

Across the road there was a toilet and an open bathroom for men near the *bhandara* premises.

There were two tents, one for eating and the other for resting, set up besides a Shiv temple-like enclosure, with *bhajans* to Lord Shiv playing, a trademark of every *bhandara* in the Amaranth Yatra circuit.

The yatris from all the six buses ate here, some men bathed, others recharged their mobiles, and relaxed. Besides the regular food, there was a *golgappa* stall which was the centre of attraction. And yes, someone handed me a Dussehri mango too!

As we relaxed in the pandal, I got to know some of the many groups who were also going to Amaranth with us. A *jethani* and *devrani*, a landlady and tenant, a group of five female friends, a group of three sisters, aunt and niece, and other families with accompanying men folk.

At 1 pm we headed for Pahalgam. One of the

strangest sights on the way to Pahalgam is one-and-a-half bogies of a train with an engine-like box parked at the side of the highway, near Banihal town. We would have loved to stop there and click pictures but we were in a rush to reach Pahalgam before night.

And after this came the surprise of all surprises. A tunnel by the name of Jawahar Tunnel, 2.547 kms long. There were emergency phones throughout the tunnel at very short distances. The 2.5 kms run was lit up by electric lights. The ride through the tunnel was exhilarating, thrilling and a bit scary! Just after you cross the tunnel is your reward—a signboard proclaiming: Welcome to Kashmir Valley.

As we entered the Kashmir valley, I was taken aback at the lush green vegetation of the valley. For a long stretch, the picture postcard valley scene did not end, and to me they seemed like green castles from a fairytale book with their many tall trees.

We then crossed the toll gate for the road ahead at Qazigund, Maikot where there are toilets and basic grocery including fresh vegetable and fruits.

As we were only a few kilometers outside the town of Pahalgam, we could see beautiful, double or triple-storey houses with sloping roofs and an abundance of windows, lining the highway.

It seemed that Kashmiri farmers had good taste in homes and were affluent. It was the growing season for rice, and the fields were full of green paddy floating in wet pond beds. We could also see military men with their guns, guarding the highway. Men and women in *phirans* walked by and we crossed a park with flowers in bloom and an excited crowd of visitors.

The Lidder river was part of our trip as it gushed and flowed over rocks, never stopping. The river flows through Pahalgam and could be seen even at Baltal, on our return journey.

When we were about 8 kms away from Pahalgam, we got our first glimpse of snow-clad mountains. So far, it had been just green mountains. At this sight, the bus exploded with joy and the *goonj* of *Bam Bam Bhole*! was once again heard. It then began to drizzle, a phenomenon which is so much part of any visit to Kashmir.

We finally reached Pahalgam at around 7 pm in the evening.

It was still daylight and as the buses parked at the parking area, just a few yards away from the Nunwan base camp for Amaranth yatris, we saw a most spectacular sight – that of snow-topped green mountains in a circle around the parked buses and other vehicles. There was a chill in the air.

We now had to pack one bag, which would last us throughout the entire Yatra to Amaranth, as we would have to travel light and carry this bag on our shoulders, for two to three days depending on how fast one could make the trip, to and fro.

Everyone got busy in packing that one special bag, changing into trekking gear and assembling all the items needed for the trek. The remaining luggage was kept in the bus storage. Clutching on to our special sticks, we marched towards the Nunwan base camp.

The Nunwan base camp buzzes with life. As we crossed security, we saw a CRPF Control Room with men in uniform guarding it. There was also a medical check up centre, an Information Centre, rooms for officials and others, all in tents.

A huge board displayed information about the camp site and some basic information. I read that there were 270 toilets, 782 tents and 13 *bhandaras* in the campus.

We stopped at the first *bhandara*, crossing little shops selling everything from curios of the Yatra to basic apparel items, required for the Yatra. In case you forgot to pack an extra pair of socks, mittens, gloves, sweater, jackets, you could buy it all here.

Post dinner, we walked out of the camp towards the main market area. By now it was dark, but the rushing Lidder river kept us company and its gurgling sound remained throughout our walk. We finally took a mini bus and stopped at Chandanwari road, where we stayed in a private hotel, belonging to a native Kahsmiri family.

It was here that the real bond of a close group of bus yatris were formed as we spent two nights here.

We were to start for Chandanwari the next morning, but news tricked in that the entry was not yet open as the arrangement by the government for tents had been delayed due to bad weather. This change in our itinerary proved to be a blessing as we got an opportunity to explore Pahalgam the next day.

On the 24th morning, I got up early, and after freshening up, walked out of the Kashmiri home to explore the area. There was a wonderful view of the mountains and at six in the morning, there was already a hustle bustle of both Yatris and the natives.

As everyone in our group of around 20 people got ready, we walked towards the base camp.

We had walked just a little distance, when, to our surprise we came across the Poshwan Park. It has a nominal entrance fee and is very elaborate and full of greenery, flower beds, especially roses, and a huge variety of other flowers. The topiary was unique. On one tall bush we found 'Allah' and on another 'Om'. We took many photographs with the backdrop of the mountain peaks.

We crossed the main market of Pahalgam, where the most common item on sale was apparels of Kashmiri embroidery and *shawls* and *phirans*, which are by now world famous for their fine and colorful yarn and neat embroidery.

We managed to get a SUV on the way and

reached Nunwan base camp. Right at the entrance of the camp was a big hoarding welcoming the yatris. Along side that was another board with the Dos and Don'ts for yatris.

Registration

Get the registration done about a month ahead of the date fixed for the commencement of the Yatra.

DOs

- Prepare for the Yatra by being physically fit.
  - ⇨ It is advisable to start a preparatory Morning/ Evening walk, of about 4-5 km per day, atleast a month prior to the Yatra.
  - ⇨ With a view to improving oxygen efficiency of the body, it may be useful to start deep breathing exercise and Yoga, particularly Pranayam.
- As the Yatra involves trekking at an altitude of 14,800 ft, do have yourself medically examined for the journey. For obtaining a Yatra Permit, a Yatri is required to furnish the prescribed compulsory Health Certificate, issued by a Registered Medical Practitioner, along with filled-in Application Form.
- Embark on the Yatra only after obtaining a valid Yatra Permit after due registration as per the procedure prescribed by the SASB, the Amarnath Shrine Board.
- You have to trek through high mountains, facing strong cold winds.

- ⇨ Do carry woolen clothing, a small umbrella (which covers the head with elastic around forehead and supported by a strap around the chin), wind-cheater, raincoat, sleeping bag, waterproof shoes, torch, stick with proper hand grip, cap (preferably monkey cap), gloves, jacket, woolen socks and trousers.
- ⇨ These are essential as the climate is unpredictable and changes abruptly from sunny weather to rain and snow.
- ⇨ The temperature may sometimes abruptly fall to 5 degrees Celsius or lower.

- For Women: Salwar kameez, pant-shirt or a track suit will be more comfortable for yatris.
- Make sure that the ponywalla, the labouror, the dandiwalla, the men and boys assisting you, are properly registered and carrys an ID Card.
  - ⇨ You can get these allotted at rates fixed by the local administration, at the camps at Baltal, Nunwan (Pahalgam), Panchtarni etc.
  - ⇨ Keep the porters and horses/ ponies with your luggage alongside as it may be difficult to trace them in case you get separated from them. This is necessary as you may suddenly need something from your luggage.
- During the Yatra from Pahalgam/Baltal onwards keep your clothes and eatables in a suitable water proof bag to avoid the belongings getting wet.
- Carry sufficient money to pay for your accom-

modation at base camps and at other stations enroute to the Holy Cave and for meeting other personal requirements.

- To enable urgent necessary action in case of any emergency, please keep in your pocket a note containing the name/address/mobile telephone number of any Yatri proceeding for *darshan* on the same date as you are going. Also carry your identity card/ driving license and your Yatra Permit issued by the SASB.
- Carry all the medicines which you take daily and, also some general medicines such as Glucose, Disprin, Move/Iodex etc.
- Carry a water bottle, dry fruits, roasted, baked grams/channa, toffees, sufficient chocolates, etc. for use during the journey.
- Keep some cold cream/ vaseline/ sun Screen with you to protect the skin from the cold winds/ sun.
- To have clear vision on sunny days, keep dark glasses / goggles handy.
- While trekking, relax for a short while every now and then on steep inclines and don't exert yourself beyond your normal capacity.
- The best way to perform the Yatra is to maintain a slow and steady pace. You will unnecessarily exhaust/tire yourself by walking fast.
- Provide all help to fellow Yatris, traveling with you and perform Yatra with a pious mind.
- Yatris are advised to strictly follow the instruc-

tions issued by the Yatra administration from time to time.

- Earth, water, air, fire, and sky are integral parts of Lord Shiv. The base camps and the entire Yatra routes are the abode of Shri Amarnathji. You must, therefore, respect the environment and do nothing whatsoever to pollute it. Use of Plastic is strictly banned and punishable under law.
- Cash offerings should be put in donation boxes of Shrine Board only.
  ⇨ You may also prefer to donate through its website.

DON'Ts

- Don't stop at places which are marked by warning notices.
- Use latrines / bathrooms in camps erected by Shri Amarnathji Shrine Board. Don't defécate in the open.
- Don't smoke and don't carry/consume any kind of narcotic or alcoholic substance.
- The Yatra is a tough trek. Small children should not undertake this Yatra.
- Women must not wear saris on this Yatra.
- Don't use slippers because there are steep rises and falls on the route to the Holy Cave. Wear shoes with laces.
- Don't attempt any short cuts on the route as doing so would be dangerous.

⇨ Do not break traffic discipline or try to overtake others in difficult stretches of the route.

- Do not do anything during the entire Yatra which could cause pollution or disturb the environment of the Yatra area. Use of polythene is banned in the state and is punishable under law.
- Do not touch or tamper with Holy Lingam and / or place or throw anything on the Holy Lingam.

  ⇨ Do not use flash cameras inside Cave.

  ⇨ Do not light incense sticks (*agarbatties*) or *dhoop* inside cave.
- Do not pay more than the prices fixed for porters, ponies, dandies, rations, fire wood, accommodation etc.
- Do not pay more for helicopter service than the rates displayed.
- Don't stay overnight at the Holy Cave due to low oxygen.

As it was the last day before the Yatra was to begin, there was heavy checking at the entrance as every year there is a fear of militant attack.

This time we stopped at the *bhandara* from Ambala. We were treated to stuffed *paranthas* with *aloo sabzi* and *rajma*.

Quoting the Chief Executive Officer of the Shrine Board, Navin K Choudhary, authorities said that on the first day of commencement of registration as many as 16,553 people had utilized the e-registration facility and the 174 bank branches for registering the dates and routes on which they wished to perform this year's Amarnath Yatra, scheduled to commence on June 25, 2012. The SASB said the registration through internet based e-registration facility through the JK Bank's website and at its branches had begun on May 7 while registration through 100 post offices had begun on May 15, 2012. Of the 16,553 yatris who had e-registered, 7,972 had opted for the traditional Pahalgam route and 8,581 had chosen the Baltal route.

The officials said they expected the number to cross last year's record of 6.3 lakh.

SK told us that the Shri Amarnath Shrine Board had increased online registration quota for pilgrims willing to undergo the religious voyage to the Cave Shrine after getting huge public response of its registration via its internet initiative.

Over 3.5 lakh people had registered since May 7 for the annual Yatra in 2012.

At a review meeting, SASB had decided to release an additional quota for online registration through the JK Bank website.

The move was made after it was observed that online registration has been most favoured and found convenient by the pilgrims.

The SASB opened on-the-spot registration counters after a large number of unregistered pilgrims arrived at the Pahalgam and Baltal base camps on the eve of the pilgrimage.

"Hundreds of unregistered yatris managed to sneak through the security barricades set up by the police and CRPF en route the cave shrine. Stopping such a huge number of people would have led to law and order problem," a sources said.

Naveen Chaudhury admitted that on-the-spot registration counters were opened, but said there was no question of allowing unregistered pilgrims for the Yatra.

While four counters had been opened in Kashmir – at Nunwan, Chandanwari, Baltal and the Tourist Reception Centre, Srinagar, two counters were opened in Jammu.

"There were some problems on the first day of the pilgrimage, but not a single unregistered yatri has been allowed to proceed towards the Holy Cave after that," Chaudhury told the media.

Chaudhury appealed to the Yatris not to embark on the pilgrimage without securing a valid registration, as this might cause inconvenience not only to themselves but also to the other Yatris.

The Amarnath Yatra 2012 was flagged off on 24th June, from Jammu amid tight security. The routes were from Pahalgam in Anantnag district and Baltal in Ganderbal district.

Stringent security arrangements had been made to ensure that the Yatra was peaceful. New security measures had been introduced in 2012, which included installation of CCTV cameras and X-ray machines for checking the baggage of pilgrims and tourists visiting this south Kashmir resort.

Barricades and check points had been created at several places along the two routes to ensure that only registered pilgrims proceeded to the holy Cave Shrine, located at an altitude of 3,880 metres.

Although the Shri Amarnath Shrine Board (SASB) had doubled its efforts to clear the track for the Amarnath Yatra 2012, the inclement weather that persisted until two days before the Yatra commenced, made some stretches dangerous for trekking, an official said.

It was found that the Cave Shrine and the stretch between Sheshnag and the Mahagunus pass, which is at 14,500 feet above sea level, was covered with thick snow even on June 22-23. Yet, the officials were confident the pilgrimage would start as scheduled, but their optimism rested on the hope that the tracks would be cleared before June 25.

"Weather conditions can change in a matter of minutes at such heights," an official said. Combined with unpredictable weather and lack of oxygen at that altitude, the snow could multiply the dangers for pilgrims proceeding on a steep and slippery track, he added.

Governor NN Vohra, said: "Our prime concern is that the pilgrims should travel comfortably and that there should not be a single loss of life."

The spirit of the yatra was at its peak as the Chandanwari entrance was to open the next day. There was a lot of mediapersons taking videos of the yatris and enquiring about their fervor for Bhole. I had carreied my notebook and was busy scribbling when I was told that my daughter and I were caught on Star TV. I found that a little amusing but left it at that.

Right in front of the *bhandara* was a truck parked with large cooking utensils and sacks of vegetables and other dry grocery items needed for providing food on a daily basis in the *bhandara*.

Behind the seating arrangement of the *bhandara* was an open kitchen where cooking was done. The *sevadhars* stayed inside the camp itself.

On our way out of the Nunwan base camp, I picked up a few booklets on Amarnath, including one on the *Amar Katha*.

It was now time to cross the highway and sit on the banks of the Lidder river. It was a bright sunny day without rain and we spent close to three hours enjoying the cool breeze, the greenish white mountains and the gurgling sound of the Lidder.

Needless to say everyone got busy posing,

clicking photographs and getting their feet wet in the cold water of the Lidder.

Meanwhile on the road, outside the camp, a group of youth, marched along with drums, eventually stopping by at the Lidder near us. Ponies and tempos were unloading mattresses in massive numbers to accommodate the inflow of yatris. Uniformed men in police jeeps ran around executing important tasks.

Once we had enjoyed the Lidder to our heart's content, we walked towards the Nunwan camp for lunch. But by now there was strict security and we were not allowed to enter the camp as the date on the registration papers for many of us was beyond the 26th. We thought best not to argue and came back from the security checkpoint to our hotel.

Just as we were leaving, a media person with a mike and videographer stopped us. We were four women, I, my daughter and two of my fellow yatris. He interviewed both the women and turned to me and asked me to tell him my name, my city and my reason for the Yatra.

I introduced myself and told the camera I had come from Faridabad. Since I had my jotting book in my hand and I had already signed the contract for my book with my publisher, I decided to reveal the true reason for my notebook always accompanying me. I told him I was here to have *darshan* of the Barfani Baba and share my experiences in the form of a book.

'So, how is your enthusiasm, in view of the weather?' he enquired.

'As far as the weather is concerned, whatever be the condition, I want to go for it. Come what may.'

'How high is your enthusiasm in the face of bad weather?' he insisted.

'My enthusiasm is very much intact and soaring,' I replied.

We then started walking back towards our Kashmiri home.

Since the walk back from the Nunwan base camp to our hotel at Chandanwari road was a considerable distance we ideally wanted to get a bus or a SUV, but no one would stop. As a result, we walked the entire length back to our hotel.

On the way we stopped to buy plums. It was here that we bumped into our Faridabad Uncle once again, who was buying shawls for his family.

After lunch we rested in the Kashmiri home and soon it was time for dinner. As we waited for dinner to be served, it dawned on me that time was running out. Early next day we were to leave for Chandanwari. Suddenly nervousness gripped me. Food was the last thing on my mind and before I knew it, tears started flowing down my cheeks.

We were in a group with some young boys and I tried hard not to cry, but the tears wouldn't stop for a while. I said nothing to anyone, but my daughter understood my dilemma.

It was my sixth sense working. Those tears were a premonition. A premonition of things to come. For the next 48 hours were the most unimaginable hours of my life that would shake me to the core of my being, to my very soul.

The Darshan

It was decided that we would get up at four in the morning and leave for Chandanwari by mini bus at 5 am, keeping in mind that 20 of us had to get ready and assemble for the Yatra.

But when it was around 2.30 am, I felt a movement in the hall we were sleeping in. One of the women was getting ready for a bath. It was difficult for me to sleep now. So I too picked up my fresh set of clothes and proceeded to bathe.

I took my time to get ready in the dim light as I wanted to start the Yatra on an auspicious note. One by one, the other members also got ready and finally at 5 am, we boarded the mini bus and set forth for Chandanwari.

So, what is it about Amaranth that made pilgrims take this difficult trek for the *darshan* of the Shivling? Just how difficult it would be, I would discover in the next five to six hours. But I was full of curiosity.

Lord Shiv's abode is the Himalayas, particularly the Kailash Parbhat. So what was the significance of Amarnath? What was special about the route earmarked for the Yatra?

As we made our way in the mini bus, there was a jam and we had to stop at a few stops in the first leg of the journey. The boys used this time to buy *namkeen* as no one had had breakfast. We skipped breakfast to avoid the rush at Chandanwari. The first day of the Yatra was 25 June and there was tremendous inflow of *yatris,* eagerly awaiting to start the Yatra.

By now, there were indications that the weather this year was bad. Just how bad, we were to discover soon.

This year, a lot of new initiatives had been started by the Amaranth Shrine Board.

To begin with, there was the mandatory registration with filling up of two forms, one general and one medical, along with five photographs. In return we were given cards with four sub cards.

On 4 June, to invoke blessings of Amaranthji for smooth Yatra of the devotees, the CEO of the Amarnath Shrine Board had performed prayer and *pooja* on the auspicious occasion of *Jayesht Purnima* at Chandanwari, at the traditional Pahalgam Holy Shrine amidst chanting of Vedic mantras.

The Meteorological department set up three Advance Weather Systems(AWS) at Sheshnag, Panchtarni and the Holy Cave from 20th June.

Many civil service and police officials were deployed at Chandanwari, Sheshnag, Pahalgam, Sangam, Holy Cave and Baltal from 14 June onwards till the end of the Yatra on 2 August. They supervised the arrangements and facilities being set up for the pilgrims, monitored the Yatra on an hour to hour basis and furnished reports to the Amarnath Shrine Board control room, five times a day at fixed hours.

On 15 June, the Amarnath Shrine Board set up a control room, equipped with a 24-hour Helpline, to facilitate the movement of the *yatris* to the pilgrimage site.

BSNL provides connectivity in the entire Yatra area. Since all the *yatris* do not use BSNL, BSNL agreed to provide pre-paid SIM cards with roaming facilities. These SIM cards were sold at special counters at the Nunwan and Baltal base camps. The SIM card was operational only for four days covering the duration of the Yatra.

All the above information was given in the official website of the Board.

So, this Yatra was indeed special and the administration seemed to understand the sentiments of the *yatris* very well.

Chandanwari is about 16 km from Pahalgam. Chandanwari is a very beautiful valley at the meeting point of hilly streams and is at a height of about 9,500 feet above sea level. The big attraction here is the snow bridge on the Lidder river.

It is believed that Lord Shiv brought forth chandan or sandal wood out of his forehead here.

As we moved towards Chandanwari by mini bus, veterans of the Yatra pointed out the Betaab valley, where the shooting of the film *Betaab* had taken place.

It took us nearly two hours to reach the base camp at Chandanwari. And here the crowd seemed endless. There was a sea of people just waiting to begin the Yatra. Vendors were selling sticks, whose importance we were to realize soon.

The authorities kept us waiting almost for half an hour before batches of *yatris* were allowed to go past the entry gate. Once inside, we had to proceed for a security check. After the security check, we waited for the rest of our group members to reach there.

As we waited for our group members, we recalled more instructions given by the Amarnath

Shrine Board: No cigarettes, no plastic, no slippers and no saris either please, the Shri Amarnath Shrine Board (SASB) again issued a detailed list of dos and don'ts for pilgrims.

In its renewed advisory for pilgrims trekking to the high altitude shrine, the SASB said: "The *yatris* must respect the pristine environment and do nothing whatsoever to pollute it.

"Use of plastic is strictly banned and punishable under the law. The *yatris* are advised to use toilets in the camps established by the Board."

Pilgrims, it added, "must neither smoke nor carry/consume any kind of narcotic or alcoholic substance. They are advised not to use slippers, because there are steep rises and falls on the route to the holy cave. "They must wear shoes with laces and not attempt any short cuts on the route as doing so would be dangerous. They must not break traffic discipline or try to overtake others in difficult stretches of the track."

The pilgrimage, it pointed out, traverses through high mountains and devotees must carry "adequate woolen clothing, a small umbrella, wind-cheater, raincoat, sleeping bag, waterproof shoes, torch, walking stick with a proper hand grip, cap (preferably a monkey cap), gloves, jacket, woolen socks and trousers".

The advisory also said, "The climate is unpredictable and changes abruptly from sunny weather to rain or snow and the temperature may sometimes abruptly fall to 5 degrees Celsius or lower."

I was aghast to see children as small as 5 or 6 years old inside the Yatra base camp.

Once all of us had arrived inside, we proceed to go further inside. Here a number of *bhandaras* were there, and one *bhandara* was continuously inviting *yartis* to savour hot *gulab jamun* and *kheer*.

We made our way to the *bhandara* and although there was a rush here, I got hold of a *kheer dona*. I handed this to my daughter and reached out for another one for myself. Even as I began to drink the *kheer*, I felt someone push against me and the *kheer* spilled, trailing down to my sweater.

The rush was making me a bit uncomfortable, but I held on to my enthusiasm and walked ahead using my stick. Once again we waited for the others to arrive. In the mean time, someone brought *samosa*. I took a bite of the *samosa* as I was beginning to feel a bit nauseous with all the excitement in the crowd.

We proceeded further and someone handed me a packet with white powder inside.

'Glucose' said my fellow *yatri*. As I quickly shoved the packet inside my sling bag, I did not realize that this would be the most important item that the tour operator had asked us to pack.

SK had arrived and it was now time to hire horses.

We had to move with the crowd, we had no choice. As soon as the horsemen came to know we required horses, they gheraoed SK and us. And then began a duel of bargaining. Ten minutes and the price was agreed upon and later it was decided that my daughter and I would move in a group of five horses.

Amid this excitement, I felt someone pat me on the back. As I looked around, I couldn't believe my eyes. It was my family doctor from my sector. I had got my Medical signed from him and knew that he was a frequent *yatri* to both Amaranth and Vaishno Devi.

We were both in a rush and with a wave he disappeared into the crowd. I finally sat on the horse, ready to begin the much awaited Yatra.

Barely had we walked seven steps when one of the five members of our group fell flat from his horse.

Aghast, I looked at him. He slowly got up and climbed up again on the horse.

Three minutes later, it began to drizzle. I could see other *yatris* putting on their raincoats. So we had to get off the horses, don our raincoats and climb up again.

As I walked ahead, I found that the majority of the *yatris* wore two-piece raincoats, one top piece and one, the rainproof legging, while both my daughter and I had the old fashioned one-piece raincoat, which unfortunately did not cover our legs. But there was no time to ponder and so we simply moved on.

Five minutes later there was yet another security check and we had to get down again.

This business of getting down from the horse and climbing up again at such short intervals was beginning to get to me. But rules were rules.

Once again, the horseman found us and we climbed back for our trek to Pissu Top.

The path to Pissu Top is serpentine, stony and zigzag, with many curves. It is about 14,000 feet above sea level.

As we started the trek, I was alarmed to see how steep the path was. The fact that the pathway was extremely rocky and uneven made the climb difficult. Just then a Kashmiri native came up and said, 'Do you need a helper? The trek is very steep and arduous.'

It took me just three seconds to decide that yes, both my daughter and I needed a helper. Not only would he carry our bags, but give us support as we scaled the rocky mountain, and when we walked, he would make way for us in the narrow pathway which was crowded with other horses and people trekking on foot.

Every time I caught my breath at the uneven jolt and had the sensation of falling off from the horse, I consoled myself that I was on the horse and had a helper. There were others facing more difficult situations. I would look far ahead at the winding, visible trail of people ahead of me and tell myself calmly: If they can do it, so can you. You are here on a mission. You can't afford to give up. This is just the beginning.

So I steadied my breath and my nerves and held on tightly to the saddle, hoping that we would successfully scale this mountain.

Uncle had told me that Pissu Top *chadai* was by far one of the most difficult of the entire trek to the Amaranth Cave.

On the way, I passed by Uncle and a few other members from our bus.

All this while, it was drizzling. My legs and feet were exposed to the rain while my torso was protected by the raincoat.

We had been climbing for about forty minutes when the scenario changed in a flash. Until now we had been climbing over the rocks, but all of a sudden there was a muddy waterfall on the path. I was totally caught off guard at this unusual sight. You can well imagine how risky the whole trek became. The muddy waterfall over the track refused to end, and we had no choice but to keep moving ahead over this. Every minute, I anticipated a fall, but not a single *yatri* fell down. Some trekkers on foot took short breaks, but no one was falling.

I kept my fingers crossed and waited for this dangerous trek to end. But it seemed endless. Every time I looked ahead I would see a line of people ahead of me, at a much higher altitude.

All this while the rain continued. By now I was beginning to feel the dampness through my leggings.

And then a thought crossed my mind. This trek was like a Death Dance. It is strange that I associated the word death with Pissu Top, although I knew nothing of its history then. It was only when I returned to Faridabad that I read about the entire Yatra route in one of the booklets I had bought form the Nunwan camp in Pahalgam.

In the *Puranas*, one finds a story: That once upon a time gods and demons came here to pay obeisance to Lord Shiv. While climbing the mountain, they grew envious of each other and began to quarrel and fight. With the blessings of Lord Shiv, the gods succeeded in destroying the demons. The heap of bones of the dead was so big that it began to look like a peak of some mountain. It is this very peak that is now called Pissu Top.

It is believed that this place has the magic power of destroying the sins of devotees of Lord Shiv.

Finally, when it seemed the end of this trek would not come, we reached a plateau-like area and the last leg of this trek was comfortable. Just then we approached a *bhandara* and stopped for refreshments, as we had not had lunch.

I was beginning to feel very cold and there was a big rush in the *bhandara*. I stayed by the bags and asked my daughter to get some refreshments. A minute later, we were joined by SK and two other tour members.

After *poori* and *chana dal sabzi*, and some *aloo tikki*, we set off again. It was the incessant rains that made things uncomfortable. For a long time we trekked and passed by Zojibal. I wanted to take a break here, but SK insisted that we continue as the weather was unpredictable and we wanted to reach Sheshnag on time.

So the trek continued and so did the rain.

Fifteen minutes later, we were told horses with riders were not allowed ahead and we had to walk. I was aghast at this piece of information. I found it difficult to walk uphill, especially with wet clothes and having been on horseback for long, it was next to impossible for me to walk. I walked a few steps and announced, 'I cant walk'.

Just then three men came running, exclaiming, '*Palki chahiye*?'

It took me a little while to understand that a *palki* was my only option for this short distance.

I once again told my daughter I needed a *palki*.

'But there is none here Mum', she said. 'Why don't you try to walk?'

'I can't', I insisted.

Just then a *palki* with a man sitting in it stopped in front of me. He was middle-aged and wet. The men were wrapping a shawl around him. He was shivering form the cold.

This *palki* moved on and in a matter of two minutes, another *palki* appeared in front of me from nowhere.

Immediately I asked, 'how much?'

'1500.'

'1200.'

'No' came the reply.

The next instant, I said. 'OK 1500' and promptly sat in the *palki* and we started moving ahead.

Just before I left, my daughter came up to me with a friend. This friend was an athlete named Ankit Dewan and an accomplished sportsman. I signaled to him to take care of my daughter. He nodded in assent and I heaved a sigh of relief. My daughter would be taken care of. I just had to handle myself.

I had never sat in a *palki* and could not imagine what lay ahead. The path was very narrow and rocky and we were thousands of feet above the valley where the Lidder was flowing, bound by snow-capped mountains with patches of old, hard frozen snow.

As the *palki* made its way, at moments it came dangerously close to the edge of the path and with four men and eight feet searching for a foothold on the paths, the *palki* rocked many times. And before I knew it, I had started wailing,

'Walk in the middle!' 'Walk in the middle'.

The balance was terrible and I was beginning to get very scared and making all sorts of noises as I imagined myself falling into the deep ravine below.

I realized, to my dismay, that my cries were drawing peoples' attention and I was setting a bad example for other *yatris*. Moreover, my cries were making the palkimen edgy, which could have proved fatal, given the treacherous path. So I did the next best thing I could have done under the circumstances. I shut my eyes, chanted *Om Namah Shivy* and surrendered my fate to Lord Shiv.

Now that my eyes were shut, I sailed through the trek in spite of the jolts.

Ten minutes later, the men put the *palki* down. My relief knew no bounds. As I paid them, they asked for *baksheesh* which I gave happily. I heaved a sigh of relief, and waited for my horse.

All the while the rain had not stopped. The continuous trek in the rain was beginning to tell on me. My reserves of energy and tolerance were reducing by the minute.

Once again I climbed on the horse and moved ahead. As I sat on the horse, my senses began to go numb. My body had started to shiver and my hands and feet were half frozen. But that was not the least of my worries. As I sat on the horse, mechanically moving ahead, I said to myself: 'This is not easy. In fact this is extremely difficult. Will I make it to the *gufa*? will I get *darshan* of the Shivling?'

My thoughts raced. There were people in my

bus like SK who had been coming here for a decade, and few others on their third or fourth trip and a few like me for the very first time.

'All I want is just one *darshan*,' I prayed to Lord Shiv, my eyes gazing blankly ahead as I moved along, not knowing what would happen in the near future.

And then we reached a little shed. A place to rest. As I climbed down from the horse, I was cold, tired and numb from the incessant rain, the difficult trek and breathless due to the high altitude.

And just then, SK was in front of me.

'Difficult?', He asked me

I did not have the strength to talk. With a finger, I pointed to my wet clothes and then raised a finger towards the sky, telling him it was the combination of wet clothes and incessant rain which drained all my energy.

It was a relief to sit on a chair and catch my breath. I bought a bottle of *limca* and sipped it to calm down. Just then, the family doctor, too, appeared out of nowhere. He had been coming here for many years and he knew it was my first trip.

Without saying a word, he handed me a packet of glucose. I quickly took a mouthful and washed it down with sips of limca.

A few minutes later I felt a bit better, though my body was still shivering with the cold. I saw my daughter and the athlete also make their way into the covered shed.

Once again, with a gesture of the hand, I pointed towards my daughter and made a silent request to the athlete who was our bus member, to take care of my daughter. Once again he nodded silently.

Which place is this? I enquired from my horseman.

We were just about 3 km from Sheshnag, I was told. It was a relief to hear this. The rain had stopped. By now I had my rest and I was ready to trek ahead.

I went up to my horseman and said, 'Hurry and take me quickly to Sheshnag. The rain has stopped thankfully.'

And so we all trotted off once more.

A little while later, I heard my fellow *yatri* calling me from the back: 'This is the Sheshnag Lake.'

I looked in awe at the serene, placid lake nestled down below, flanked by the snowy mountains which reminded me of Shiv.

Seshnag symbolizes the cosmic ocean in which Lord Vishnu, the preserver of this universe, moves, reclining on a seven-headed mythical snake.

There was as steely silence, a quiet aura emanating from the lake. I looked at it transfixed. Another symbol of Lord Shiv.

As long as we passed by it, I could not take my eyes off. Sitting high above on the horse, I could sense how icy cold the still waters must be.

And then my fellow *yatri* said, 'Look, the Lidder starts from this lake.'

I squinted my eyes and looked hard. Sure enough. I hadn't noticed this till he pointed out the source of the river. From one end of the lake emerged a narrow river, which was none other than the Lidder. I found it a bit strange that out of the placid water, a stream ran forth, gurgling and moving energetically all the way from here to Pahalgam and still farther, till Baltal. As stunned as I was by the day's unexpected events due to a number of unimaginable factors, I found this an anomaly in geography. Perhaps I was wrong, but that is what crossed my mind as I looked down.

The lake remained in view for a long time and then the path swerved and we lost sight. We had almost reached the Sheshnag camp. While we were a few yards away, and I was about to get down from the horse, suddenly I was full of emotion. The entire day's experience had Lord Shiv in every moment.

From the steep trek at Pissu Top, the gushing muddy waters and the Dance of Death, the fear of falling twice from the horse, the fright in the *palki*, the lofty, snow-capped mountains, the chill and shivering in my body and the deceptive calmness of the Sheshnag lake. In that instant I knew I had felt the tremors of Lord Shiv. And as this realization sank in, I started crying. Deep sobs shook my body and grew louder by the minute. I tried hard to control the tears and the sound but couldn't. The cries threatened to turn into shrieks and howls had I not controlled myself all this while, holding on tightly to the saddle with both my hands.

The helper and the horseman were visibly disturbed to see me in this state.

'Didi, why are you crying? Please don't cry. We all have to die one day.'

At last I quietened down and found my voice.

I wiped my tears, 'I am not scared of dying.'

I was not scared of dying, I assured them.

'You wont understand', I added.

'What?' The helper asked.

Didi is saying, 'you wont understand',repeated the horseman.

And after that we were all quiet.

Finally it was time to get down.

As I paid the horseman and the helper, both asked for *baksheesh*.

I was already running short of funds. I had spent extra on hiring the helper at three intervals. I had not anticipated the expense of a *palki*. And I needed to buy warm clothes.

'You will get *baksheesh*, once I have the *darshan*', I said. The purpose and the goal was not yet achieved, I added.

After paying both, the horseman and the helper, I walked towards the Sheshnag camp where

I saw SK, my daughter, the athlete and a few other members of our group.

Sheshnag lake is at a distance of about 15 km from Chandanwari. It is the second camp on the way to Shri Amarnath. It is about 11,730 feet above sea level. There are three beautiful peaks – Brahma, Vishnu, Mahesh – that stand near the lake.

Without uttering a word, SK handed me a bottle containing an orange liquid. Instinctively I knew it was Glucon C, as Sheshnag is known to have low amount of oxygen and it is normal for many *yatris* to feel breathless. I drank mouthfuls of Glucon C, which made me feel better.

I was bone tired, cold, shivering and ready to drop dead but glad that we had come almost half way for the Yatra. There was only one thing I needed at this point. A3 ft by 6 ft space to rest my tired body.

As we walked past the tents I said to SK, 'I need to lie down on a mattress.'

He nodded in assent and went to book tents for our group.

My clothes were soaking wet, waves of shivering raked my body. I knew I needed warm clothes, or else I would fall sick. I was mighty happy to see a shop selling Yatra items. I stopped by this shop to buy a warm body suit, a thick jacket, gloves, socks and a pair of trekking shoes.

I managed to trudge on the snowy path, with the help of my stick and when SK pointed to our tent, I quickly removed my soiled shoes and dropped dead on the soft mattress.

I lay on the mattress in my wet clothes for half an hour. While my body was fatigued, my mind was alert. I heard other members of the group coming into the tent and resting. Because of the low oxygen, a few people half my age were vomiting.

Half-an-hour of rest on the mattress was enough to give me a little strength. I knew I had to stop myself from falling ill so that I could have *darshan* of Barfani Baba. I requested SK to ask the male members in the tent to go outside for a while so that I could change into fresh clothes. But everyone was bone tired.

So, with a mattress acting as a curtain, I changed into warm clothes, buttoned up my new jacket, adjusted my monkey cap and once again lay down on the mattress. There was hardly any strength in my body but my resolve was intact. I knew I did not have the strength to walk to the *bhandara* for dinner. But I needed food to give me strength for tomorrow's trek.

So, I said to my daughter, ' I wont be going to the *bhandara*. Get me a bottle of Slice and a packet of biscuits. That will be my dinner.'

'How are you feeling now?' she asked.

'Much better in the warm clothes', I rep[lied. 'But my feet will freeze without socks.'

On hearing this, my daughter took out the new pair of socks we had bought and slipped them on my feet.

'Have some *kaju* Mum', she called out.

I did not have the strength to move my arm to eat food. 'Put it in my mouth', I told her. And she promptly did that.

Two hours later my body had some rest and the chill in my bones began to thaw. It was now time for that bottle of Slice and biscuits . I asked my daughter to give me the food packet and with her shining the torch light, I had my basic dinner. Then I fell asleep.

In the middle of the night, suddenly there was a commotion.

SK walked into the tent, shining a torch at us.

We had to accommodate two extra people in our tent. They were from Faridabad, although they were not in our group.

By now almost everyone in the tent was awake. A little shuffling, a little pulling of mattresses and quilt and space was made for two people.

The two people, a man and a woman, walked inside the tent and snuggled under the quilt.

'Remember the bridge that broke on the way to Sheshnag?'

'They got stuck there, along with a group of other *yatris*. They were helped by the military personnel to get here through an alternate pathway. That is why they reached Sheshnag just half-an-hour before.'

'I saw them sitting in the open in front of a small fire, warming their hands, shivering badly.'

'Because of the incessant rains, a greater number of *yatris* have stopped at Sheshnag', SK explained.

'I have adjusted two more members of their group in the adjacent tent.'

It was 3 am. We offered our guests some dry fruits. Then quiet descended in the tent once again.

The entire Sheshnag area is surrounded by snowy mountains. And we slept on the ice, covered with water proofing.

An hour later it was time for nature's call. I did not have the strength to go on my own, so holding on to my stick and with my daughter lending me support, I hobbled to the bathroom and back. Thankfully, it was still night and finally I dozed back to sleep.

We all got up early the next day. And we all felt better after a night's rest, even if it was in icy, low oxygen environment.

Since I had already seen the location of the toilet, this time, I went on my own. As I was about to enter one of the toilets, a fellow member from our tour said, 'Aunty it is open from one side.' The abnormality of this struck me for a minute. But it was a question of survival.

'It is ok. I'll manage, somehow,' I said.

Later, when we were back home in Faridabad, I realized we had been luckier than other female *yatris*. The *Hindustan Times* had carried a bizarre story that two teenaged boys, working in a *bhandara* at Baltal, had tried making a video of a woman yatri having a bath in a makeshift toilet, via the holes in the tin sheet. An FIR had been lodge and their mobiles had been confiscated for starters.

As we all moved out of the tents, we decided to skip breakfast as our intention was to reach the *gufas* at any cost.

'We are anticipating bad weather', someone said. As I looked upwards, clouds hung low over a mountain peak, almost touching the horizon. I stood watching transfixed and within a span of around 30 seconds, the entire mountain range surrounding the camp was covered with dark clouds, temporarily obliterating the very existence of those snowy peaks that guarded the Sheshnag lake and the camp.

Once again, I felt the presence of Lord Shiv. But I knew he would be kind and benevolent to his devotees, even if he wished to test our determination and faith.

My Nike shoes, which had brought me till Sheshnag, had to be abandoned as they were soiled beyond use.

Getting wet in the rain had given me a phobia of having to do the Yatra in the rain. So, besides warm clothes, my daughter and I had also bought two pair of raincoats with separate piece for the top and leggings.

While this worked fine for my daughter, I had reservations about mine as the legging was tight. As I walked from the tent towards the waiting horsemen, I wondered whether I would be able to climb on the horse.

As I walked towards my horse, my right foot fell in a little pool of muddy water. Ignoring this, I proceeded to climb on the horse. As I tried to lift my right leg, the raincoat came in the way. I also realized that the woolen socks my daughter had made me put on last night in the tent had made my shoes tight. The next instant I knew what was to be done. In a jiffy, I removed the raincoat legging and kept it aside. I unlaced my shoes and removed my woolen socks and hurriedly put them in my bag. I should have put on normal nylon socks, but there was no time for that. The horses had already started moving. And so did I.

As we moved out of Sheshnag, the terrain changed dramatically. Now there was nothing in sight except snow. Snow on the left, snow on the right, snow on the path and snow as far as one could see.

The temperature was dipping. I wondered what would be my fate if it again started to rain. While the top portion of my body was protected by the rain coat, my legs were exposed. I also wondered how my sockless feet would fare in the extreme weather.

Fifteen minutes on, the most unexpected thing happened. It started to snow. I couldn't believe my eyes. For someone who had the first glimpse of snow in life on this journey, the thought of witnessing a snow fall had never entered my mind. But here we were. Moving in single file as the snow gently fell on the yartris and powdered the ground.

Because we had already faced such hazards yesterday, I was not ruffled too much. Though I did wonder how long and how hard it would snow. Now every yatri had his face down, in order to prevent the snow from falling on the face. As we moved, tiny cotton-like flakes settled on my woolen leggings and on the mane of the horse, as well on the horseman's *phiran*.

We kept moving and so did everyone else. There was a strange silence in the air.

There was a hush in the atmosphere. It seemed to me that suddenly the trek had turned into a silent, mute zone, as there was pin drop silence.

My mind went back to 1996 when incessant rains had caused the glacier to burst and many yatris had lost their lives in spite of the valiant efforts of the rescue operation of the Shrine Board.

A few minutes on and the rainfall stopped abruptly. Everyone heaved a sigh of relief.

A little while later the sun appeared, bright in the sky.

And suddenly the morale of yatris was uplifted.

Jubilant chants of *Bhole ki maya, Kabhi dhoop kabhi chhaya* echoed throughout the snowy terrain.

And after that, we never encountered either rain or snow till the *darshan.*

As we were crossing the glacier, this was perhaps the most arduous part of the trek. On our way to Panchtarni, we crossed two major military camps which provided medical assistance to yatris and served warm water.

We were now on our way to Poshpatri. I had heard about this famous *bhandara* from Uncle. He had told me that this *bhandara* served an amazing variety of food items, right in the midst of glacial surroundings. He said that the food served here for the yatris could probably not be found even in an average marriage.

It was only when we landed here that I came to know that the food here was served as *chappan bhog* (56 itmes), the special foods cooked for Lord Jagannath in the coastal town of Puri. As always, whenever you enter any *bhandara*, you are greeted with songs and *bhajans* of Bhole.

The *bhandara* here is a high-rise dome structure, with stalls on both the sides, the centre serving as a eating area, with some tables and chairs on the side.

Every item has a banner, just like in a catered dinner party. I quickly scanned the array of food stalls and headed towards the *paneer tikka*. I guess it was the Punjabi in me that took me to this counter. After the trek through the glacier and the unexpected snow fall, I felt it would do wonders for my stomach. Since I love south Indian cuisine, I next went for an *idli* followed by half a *dosa*.

With the tempting array of sweet dishes, it would have been sacrilege not to sample one. So, after making a tough decision between hot *gulab jamun* and some other kind of sweets, I settled for *ras malai*. Here, a word of caution. In spite of the *chappan bhog* here, do not eat too much. Staying on a light stomach is the pr-requisite for a comfortable trek.

And then SK came and asked me: 'How do you like the ambience of this place?'

I joined my index finger with my thumb, indicating that it was simply out of this world.

'Yatris are requested not to waste even a scrap of food as it is indeed difficult to get the food brought up here', he said. It costs Rs 800 to get a gas cylinder and Rs 500 just to get one large pot here from the base camp.

Refreshment over, it was now time for the penultimate leg of the trek, to reach Panchtarni, after which we would reach our final destination the Holy Cave.

As we left Poshpatri, we also left behind the snow and entered thre range of the Mahaguna mountains. Panchtarni is about 13 kms from Sheshnag and at an altitude of 12,000 feet above sea level. Flanked by the Mahaguna mountains with their distinct brown and green colour, the valley has large open meadow-like grounds with streams running across the trekking path. Panchtarni is an important camp en route to the Holy Cave Shrine.

During the course of the Amarnath pilgrimage, there appears a temporary town of tents in the open fields of Panchtarni. It lies in the bosom of Bhairav ghati. Another interesting thing about here is that all of a sudden, the sky is full of the sounds of helicopters, going to and from here to take devotees to the destination.

From Panchtarni, the holy cave is about 6 kms. Here there are five holy streams where many pilgrims take bath and proceed further to the Holy Cave.

We did not stop at Panchtarni but moved ahead to scale the Mahagunas mountains. At a place around Ganesh Top, the ascent is very steep. What is even more amazing is that here there is usually a traffic jam. You might ask—a traffic jam? Yes, a clutter of horses and people and the military negotiating the to and fro traffic and ensuring a safe trek for the yatris.

Just as you are about 3 kms away from the cave, there stands a glacier. This path also has the Amravati stream flowing by. This stream is also known as Amar Ganga. It is here that many yatris stop to take a bath before going for *darshan*. But this year the stream was almost frozen, except for a small area where the military had cleared the frozen ice for the water to be clear for yatris to freshen up.

From here, you have to either trek on the snowy path or take a *palki*, which will take you right up to the last step of the Holy Cave.

As you start walking on the snowy pathway leading up to the Holy Cave, the entire stretch of the path is lined up with little shops selling *prasad*. These shops also have a tented area where yatris can relax and keep their luggage while going for *darshan* of the Shivling. Each shop has a number for easy accessibility, lest you forget the place where you rested and bought *prasad*.

Also available is a bucket of hot water so that you can bathe before having *darshan* of the ice Shivling.

We finally reached the first step of the stairs leading up to the Holy Cave. From here there is a plethora of military personnel and other staff to help yatris.

On reaching the first *seedhi*, we stopped by at a shop on the right, to buy *prasad*. We also deposited our bags here. The *prasad* from this shop is unique and special. It contains an exhaustive collection of items, which make for a perfect *prasad* and items to cherish long after you have returned from Amaranth.

The *prasad* box contains the flowing: *Pullian*,

makhana, dry apple, *phool makhani*, coconut, *jaap* mala, *chunrie*, *mouli*, the Amar Katha book, photograph of Holy Shivling, and *Rudraksha dana*. At the bottom of the box is a little instruction for the yatris: *Kripya is dabbe ko istmaal karne ke baad paani main pravaah kar den.* Please discard this box by floaling it in water.

Here too, one has a tendency to feel breathless, so one should keep glucose handy, lest one falls sick just a few yards away from *darshan*.

Invariably, family members get separated as some travel by *palki* and some by foot. There is an announcement centre here which helps to locate lost/and separated family or tour members.

One important piece of information. If you hire a *palki*, make sure you ask the palkiwala to give you his ID. Hang this around your neck, and pay him only when he has taken you the entire distance.

There are three stairways leading up to the Holy Cave. One is for going, the second one is for returning and the *palkiwalas*.

Such is the deep faith for Barfani Baba that old and physically unfit people too have a dream of *darshan* and you can see many old men and women going in *palkis*.

Once we had reached the first step of the stairway leading up to the *gufa*, my excitement knew no bounds. I could not believe that I had finally made it here and now *darshan* was just a matter of another 15 or 20 minutes.

Holding on to the *prasad* packet, we kept climbing the stairs, one by one, a huge crowd of people ahead of us and with the constant ringing of bells, filling us with deep reverence for Lord Shiv.

There is no man-made temple or Shivlaya here. All that one can see is the natural and uneven cave, which has neither a gate nor an entry.

The Holy Cave is about 12,730 feet above sea level and is 60 feet long, 25 feet wide and 15 feet high. It is a strange and wonderful sight, jutting on the top of a rock to find a semi- enclosure for the lingam.

The Amarnath Shrine Board curtailed this year's yatra to 39 days from 45 days in 2011, citing hostile weather conditions as the prime reason, so there was a bigger rush of yatris in the first five days of the 2012 Yatra.

The shrine forms an important part of ancient Hindu mythology.

The reference to Amarnath can be seen in the *Nilamata Purana* (v.1324).

The pilgrimage to the Holy Cave has been described with full topographical details in the *Bhringish Samhita* and the *Amarnatha Mahatmya*, ancient texts said to have been composed even earlier.

References to Amarnath has also been made in historical chronicles like the *Rajatarangini*.

Several Western travellers' accounts also leave no doubt about the fact that the Holy Cave has been known to people for centuries.

"The lake of dazzling whiteness [resembling] a sea of milk (Sheshnag), which he created [for himself as residence] on a far off mountain, is to the present day seen by the people on the pilgrimage to Amareshwara."(*Rajatarangini*, Book I v. 267. Translation: M A Stein).

The Amarnath Cave has been a place of worship since time immemorial. There are references to one Aryaraja (32BCE-17CE) who used to worship a lingam formed of ice in Kashmir. The book *Rajatarangini* (Book VII v.183) refers to Amareshwara or Amarnath.

It is believed that Queen Suryamathi in the 11th century AD gifted trishuls, banalingas and other sacred emblems to this temple. *Rajavalipataka*, by Prajyabhatta, has detailed references to the pilgrimage to the Amarnath Cave.

There are further references to this pilgrimage in many other ancient texts.

The long-standing strife in the Kashmir valley has had effects on the yatra too. Since 1989, J&K state has been under the shadow of cross-border terrorism. In 2000, thirty Amarnath piligrims were massacred by militants in Pahalgam, when they were on the way to the Amarnath Holy Cave. The attack was led by Lashar-e-Toiba (LeT). The killings were widely condemned by all sections of society.

The pilgrimage was banned from 1991 to 1995 due to threats from militants. In 1996, the militants had assured that they would not interfere, allowing a resumed yatra with far greater numbers than in previous years.

Moroever, there has been controversy regarding the land for the Shrine Board.

On 26 May 2008, the Government of India and the Government of Jammu and Kashmir reached an agreement to transfer 99 acres (0.40 km2) of forest land to the Shri Amarnathji Shrine Board (SASB) in the main Kashmir valley, to set up temporary shelters and facilities for Hindu pilgrims. This caused a controversy, with demonstrations from the Kashmir valley against the land transfer and protests from the Jammu region supporting it.

The largest demonstration saw more than 500,000 protesters at a single rally, among the largest in Kashmir's history. Such is the reverence for Barfani Baba.

On August 31, 2008, the 61-day old agitation in the Jammu region over the Amarnath land row ended with an agreement between the agitators and the J&K Governor-appointed panel. Under the terms of the agreement, the Shrine Board would be making temporary use of 40-hectares of land during the relevant Yatra period.

There is no obstacle at the mouth of the cave. One can easily enter it, it is wide and open for the yatris.Water drops continue to trickle down here and there in this Holy Cave.

It is believed that there is a Rama Kund on the mountain above this cave.

It is in this Holy Cave that Lord Shiv had narrated the Amar-katha to Parvati.

Although the existence of the Holy Cave has been mentioned in the *Puranas*, the popular story narrated by people about the re-discovery of this Holy Cave is of a shepherd, Buta Malik. The story goes like this:

A saint gave Buta Malik a bag full of coal. On reaching his home, when he opened the bag, to his utter surprise, the bag was full of gold coins. This overwhelmed him. He ran to thank the saint. But the saint had disappeared. Instead, he found the Holy Cave and the ice Shivlingam in there. He announced this discovery to the villagers. Then onward, this became a sacred place of pilgrimage.

Behind the discovery of the Holy Shrine lies yet another interesting story. Centuries ago Maa Parvati asked Shivji to let her know why and when he started wearing a garland of heads (*Mund Mala*), to which Bhole Shankar replied, 'whenever you are born, I add more heads to my bead'.

Parvati said, 'I die again and again, but you are immortal. Please tell me the reason behind this.'

Bhole Shankar replied that, 'For this, you will have to listen to the *Amar Katha*.'

Shiv agreed to narrate the detailed story to Maa Parvati.

He started searching for a lonely place where no living being could listen to the immortal secret and ultimately chose the Amarnath Cave.

In the hush-hush, he left his Nandi (the bull which he rides) at Pahalgam. It is believed that in ancient times, this place was known as Bailgaon as Lord Shiv had left his bull here. With passage of time, under the influence of the local language, this place began to be known as Bailgam and subsequently Pahalgam.

At Chandanwari, he released the Moon (Chand) from his hair.

At the banks of Lake Sheshnag, he released his snakes. He decided to leave his son Ganesha at the Mahagunas Parvat. The old name of this place was Mahaganesh which, with passage of time and under the influence of the Kashmiri language, began to be called Mahagunas.

At Panchtarni, Shivji left the Five Elements behind (Earth, Water, Air, Fire and Sky) which give birth to life and of which he is the Lord.

After this, it is believed that Lord Shiv and Maa Parvati performed the tandav dance in that mountain range. This dance symbolizes the spirit of detachment.

After leaving behind all these, Bhole Shankar entered the Holy Amarnath Cave along with Parvati Maa and took his Samadhi.

To ensure that no living being is able to hear the immortal tale, he created Kalagni and ordered him to spread fire to eliminate every living thing in and around the Holy Cave.

After this he started narrating the secret of immortality to Maa Parvati. But, as a matter of chance, a pair of pigeons overhead the story and became immortal.

According to Amar Katha Lord Shiv then blessed the gods saying,'O Gods! You have seen my Barfani linga in this cave and so you need not fear death any more. Henceforth, my linga-shaped body will be known as Amresh.'

That is why Lord Shiv was called as Amreshvar here and the holy place as Amarnath.

At the shrine, the crowd of devotees kept moving, when a shower of rain sprinkled us and my fellow yatris burst into chants of Bhole in ecstasy at having been so blessed by the Barfani Baba.

I waited amidst the crowd, finally I had reached the platform where the Shivlingam was situated. I quickly made my way through the crowd, which was an effort, and rested at the metal grill. It was indeed a moment of inexplicable joy to see the Shivlingam. I felt immense happiness as I thanked Lord Shiv for making my Yatra successful.

The Shivlingam waxes during May to August and gradually wanes thereafter. This lingam is said to grow and shrink with the phases of the moon, reaching its height during the summer mela.

The Barfani Shivlingam and the platform on which it appears are made of solid snow while outside the cave, there is semi solid snowfall around for miles together. This is indeed a very strange and unbelievable phenomenon.

I put part of the *prasad* in the small opening at the centre of the grill and moved ahead to see smaller ice stalactite of Shri Ganesha and Kartikeyaji near the Shivling.

At a little distance from it, one can see a somewhat bigger stalactitie of Maa Parvati.This is called the Parvatipeeth. It is believed that this *peeth* is one of the 51 *shaktipeetha* and that the head of Bhagwati Sati had fallen here.

So, we got *darshan* of the entire Shiv family.

According to the Amar Katha, a pair of pigeons that live here are said to be those ones that were immortlaised. How they survive in the extreme weather remain an unsolved mystery as the cave is surrounded by snowy mountains. The cave itself is covered with snow most time of the year, except for summer when it is open for pilgrims.

My daughter was some distance behind me as we were separated. She later told me she had seen the pigeons.

Once I had the *darshan*, I moved backwards

and stood there for a while, gazing at the *Shivling*, for which I had made this arduous trek, while the crowd of devotees kept moving in front of me to the chants of *Jai Bholenath ki*.

Finally, I moved towards the exit of the cave. As I came outside, there sat a sadhu, with matted hair and his body completely covered with rudraksha mala. He held a little baton and was giving a gentle blow on the head of each devotee as a blessing. I too bowed my head in front of him and he touched me with the baton.

A few chairs were there at the exit, along with a couple of military personnel. I sat down and waited for my daughter and other members to reach here and we finally made our way out, down the stairs.

I decided to go back to the horses *adda* in a *palki* while my daughter and the athlete walked back.

As I stopped at a shop to buy a bottle of mineral water, I was in for a surprise. The bottle cost more than its MRP.

This time there was no reason to feel scared, I would be sitting in the *palki* on a flat snowy road, unlike the steep rocky path, on the way to Sheshnag.

So I shut my eyes and relaxed, all the while thanking Lord Shiv for the *darshan*.

It was decided that instead of staying at the tents, we would leave the Holy Cave glacier and move to Baltal on horses.

Around ten minutes later, something snapped in the *palki* and I found myself flat on the snowy ground. Since my eyes had been shut, I had no clue as to what or how this happened.

Immediately the *palkimen* rushed to me:

Are you hurt?

I took a few seconds to compose myself. Since I had already had the *darshan*, there was a sense of peace in my mind. Had this happened on the way to the *darshan* I would have been surely perturbed.

No, I said bravely.

'How did this happen?' I asked

'Didi, my foot slipped accidently', one man replied.

'Be careful now. I am very tired and can't take any more shocks.'

'Don't worry Didi.'

And I got up and once again sat down in the palki. A few minutes later I was dropped at the spot from where we had to hire horses to Baltal.

By the time we managed to hire three horses, one each for me, my daughter and the athlete, it was past six in the evening.

I knew there was no way we could reach Baltal in daylight. But because it was my first trip, I decided to put all the decisions in the hands of people more experienced than me like SK and the athlete.

So, once again, we trotted off on the horses on our return journey to Baltal, while SK and his group of young boys decided to trek back on foot.

They assembled all their bags and gave them to a *pithoowala* who would carry the bags to Baltal.

As we set forth on our return journey, there was once again a jam on the track. There are two separate routes for going to the Holy Cave, One is the traditional route, the longer one from Pahalgam which we had taken. The other is from Baltal, which is much shorter and is relatively less difficult. At a short distance the two routes merge and it is here that the horse traffic has to be managed by a whistle-blowing military personnel.

As the horse traffic eased, we saw a whole lot of yatris coming for *darshan* in *palkis*. I noticed with a little amusement that 99 per cent of them had a dazed look on their faces, though no one uttered a word of regret, fear or any other emotion.It was faith that brought every yatri here, and no one was willing to go back without *darshan*, fear notwithstanding.

The first two-and-a-half hours passed easily as there was still natural light. But after around 8 pm, it began to get dark. I was amazed to see that there was an inflow of yatris to and fro on this route, both on foot and on horses.There was no light on the route, but the entire path ahead of me was lit up by small torches, carried by those on foot. I could not believe that yatris would risk travelling on foot in the darkness, but this was just the kind of faith yatris had on Bhole.

As we trotted along, we would see people walking with sticks, holding on to their torches, calling out to other members of their group to ensure they were close by.

After about three-and-a-half hours of our journey, the three horseman stopped at a little shack for tea. What I witnessed here left me cold. Two little girls sat at the mound crying. I could not see their faces, but their incessant cries for their parents made me squirm. They were both wearing raincoats and constantly telling their horseman that they were feeling cold and wanted to go to Mummy and Daddy.

The horseman had a tough job. He had to pacify the girls and also call out their father's name every 30 seconds.

I would have liked to do something but the helplessness of the situation made me numb, so I sat there like a dummy, witnessing the night drama. I was full of anger for the parents who did not have the foresight to avoid an unwanted situation like this.

Here, I have to confess that I am baffled how the Shrine Board allows yatris to travel in the dark, and how can they allow registration of children? *I strongly recommend that anyone below 12 years should avoid taking the Yatra,* though there was one small kid in our group and he managed without any major problem.

It was beginning to get darker and darker and the half moon in the dark star-lit sky shed no moonlight on the track. If the trek to Pissu Top reminded me of a Death Dance, this seemed like Midnight Tango.

Bade chalo, chale chalo, seemed the only thing to do.

As I faced such unexpected things on our way to the darshan I had resigned myself to Lord Shiv, happy that in a few hours we would reach the safety and sanctity of Baltal and that the Yatra had been successful, thanks to the blessings of Bhole.

Shortly before reaching Baltal, we passed a few *bhandaras* where there was an atmosphere of festivity with *bhajans* being played.

At long last, I spotted a flat ground with a few parked vehicle and I knew we had reached Baltal. It was past 10.30 in the night.

My legs were aching badly, and I nearly vowed never to sit on a horse again in my life, so tired was I with the continuous horse riding of the past two days.

I called out to the athlete, 'Have we reached Baltal?'

Yes.

Why cant we stop?

We will. Just a little further.

I am too tired

Only a little further

We were now trotting on a tar road which was undoubtedly better than the path we had crossed in the past few hours, but all my strength had dwindled. I wanted to jump off the horse and lie on the bed.

We took a slight turn and I was amazed at the sight in front of me. The entire stretch on the right side of the road, ahead of me was lit up. The brightness and the close lighting baffled me. Even in Diwali I had not seen such lights.

It dawned on me that the lights were of the *bhandaras*, since Baltal is a base camp for the Yatra. We felt as if those lights were just for us, welcoming our successful *darshan* and Yatra. And perhaps it was so.

Now that we had reached the *bhandara* I wanted to get down at the nearest one, but the athlete edged me on by saying,just a little ahead.

I can't any more.

Why can't you take me by a vehicle?

There are no local vehicles here, he replied. Only private ones.

I felt my legs would fall off from the joints, I was so tired.

A few minutes later the athlete stopped the horses and we finally got down.

Without asking him, I simply walked up to the *bhandara* opposite and sat down on a chair. I shut my eyes, not caring a bit about what anyone thought of my dishevelled appearance as my clothes had become wet and soiled by the fall from the *palki*.

It was a bliss to sit on a chair after nearly five hours on the horse. It was almost like coming home. There was an awful sense of gratefulness to Bhole and now I knew, the recovery process was just around the corner.

Among The Blessed

I don't know how long I sat on the chair. Maybe twenty minutes. Even though my eyes were shut, I could hear the sound of people talking and walking around me. As I opened my eyes, a stranger came up to me and said, 'Why don't you take medicine?'

I smiled feebly and said, 'I'll take after dinner.'

The three of us had dinner and the owner of the *bhandara,* seeing the late hour and our condition, managed to clear some space in the adjoining halls and created just enough space for the three of us.

As we moved towards our space, I saw two rows of sleeping *yatris* covered with blankets. There was something soothing about it. Perhaps I felt so, now that I knew we had left the difficult terrain and tough weather. In other words, we were now safe.

I woke up next day, early in the morning. It was a relief to know that there were proper toilets and running water in them. Also, there was a separate corner for washing up. As I brushed my teeth, I heard this *bhajan* from the *pandal*: *Parvaton ke beech main kaisa hai ye Bhola anjaana...*

After freshening up, we picked up our bags and moved out as the athlete wanted us to go to another *pandal*. This one was from Delhi and Cheeka, in Haryana. I was surprised that here, instead of a Shiv Mandir, there was a Mata Vaishno Mandir, with pictures of the *pindi darshan*. I briefly prayed to her before moving on to the next *pandal*, which was from Budhlada, a town in Mansa district in the state of Punjab.

We went to the Punjab *pandal* and sat in a corner. The athlete and my daughter went to locate other members of the group. As I sat on the chair against a round table in a corner, I reflected on the happenings of the past 24 hours. The sheer enormity of my entire experience once again brought a tear to my eye every now and then. I must have sat there over three hours, gazing towards the road in front, which never ceased to bring a lineup of either horses with horsemen or *yatris* coming back from Amaranth.

As I recalled the glittering lighting of last night, I was amazed at the *shraddha* people had for Bhole and the *yatris* and their welfare. The entire base camp was an amalgamation of *bhandaras* for the service of the *yatris*.

We had breakfast and I waited for the other members of our group to arrive.

I finally took out my camera, which I had abandoned for the past 48 hours in view of the difficult trek, and moved to the road outside the *pandal*. There was a lovely view of snow-capped mountains and I clicked away happily. A little further, opposite to the road was the Lidder river, our constant companion.

In the mean time, the cleaning man vigorously started sweeping the carpet, moving aside chairs. This over, another man put golden satin coverings on the round tables as well as the chairs. Having covered the tables and chair with golden satin, he placed maroon satin covers with lace on every table. The *pandal* already had chandeliers of flowers hanging from the roof and a couple of more of these were added.

People started walking in. It was noon and lunch was served. I was happy to see other members of the group with whom we had shared the Pahalgam hotel. We were meeting after two-and-a-half days.

All the women were overcome by the whole experience but grateful for the *darshan.*

More and more *yatris* came for lunch. We too had lunch, followed by crispy sweet *jalebis.*

Right opposite this *bhandara* was a Shiv temple. And along side was a medical camp with the message: Inspiration SABLO

I wondered what was the meaning of SABLO and asked my daughter to go find out and come back with a pamphlet, if one was available.

Before my daughter returned, a tall, well-built middle aged man walked up to me and said: SABLO stands for Shri Amaranth Barfani Langar Organization.

He introduced himself and told me that this *bhandara* was 27 yerars old. 'When I started 27 years ago, there were only three *bhandars.* One of Gulshan Kumar, of T series, one ours and one another one. Over the years, the number of *bhandaras* increased as awareness and faith increased. We have three *bhandaras.* One each in Pahalgam and Panchtarni besides this one.'

'So you come every year here with your staff?'

'Yes. We have a staff of 225 which is divided in three places.'

'Is this your first visit to Amaranth?'

'Yes.'

'Have you come alone?'

'No. I have come with my daughter. But with a group who are experienced.'

'Did you have *darshan* via helicopter?'

'No. By horses.'

'Must have been a bit expensive.'

'Yes, it was. But I wanted to experience the traditional route.'

'This is wonderful *seva* which you are doing.'

'Yes, but we don't get enough support.'

'But there is so many facilities at every step of the Yatra', I said.

'There is. But if you go deeper into this, there needs to be a lot more done.' And with a wave of his hand hc went away.

The time simply passed as we kept sitting here, relaxing, watching *yatris* come and go. I was told it was time for snacks and now an aroma of ajinomoto wafted into the *pandal*. I knew instinctively *chowmien* was on the menu, which brought a broad smile on my face. This was followed by *dosa, chaat*. But the icing on the cake was having *kulfi* here!

Now there was a long queue of people to savour the snacks. The day spent here was an antidote to the previous 48 hours and the smile on my face got bigger as the day progressed.

Dinner brought yet another surprise. The menu had *makki ki roti* and *sarson ka saag*, besides other vegetables. And this night there were two sweet dishes. *Gajar ka halwa* and hold your breath, *rabari*, which was especially being made in a corner in a huge *kadai*. Surely this was a special menu, a special day and I could not stop wondering at the *aastha* of the *bhandara* owner.

We spent the night at the camp opposite the *bhandara*. Most *bhandaras* either charge a nominal fee for a bed or none at all. Those that do not charge anything, take a deposit at night for the blankets. The deposit is returned the next morning as you return their blankets.

As we explored the Baltal road, SK told me that a *bahndara* from Jaipur near the check post was also announcing names of lost *yatris* and helping them get back to their families. In addition to this, a *bhandara* from Moradabad had taken up the task of lighting the path up to 3 km from the base towards the trek route to the shrine.

We were supposed to start for Katra on the 27th itself but because all the bus members had not arrived form *darshan*, we got one and a half-day of rest, which was very welcome.

So, around 5.30 pm, our bus started from Baltal for Katra. I thanked Uncle for all his support, happily telling him that we had had *darshan* of the Shivling. I came to know then that he was not well and had been given both medication and injection for stomach pain.

It was here that all the bus members met finally, after almost a gap of three-and-a-half days. I came to know that not everybody from our bus had had the good fortune of having *darshan* of Barfani Baba, in spite of making the arduous journey.

One of Uncle's friends, who was also from our neighbourhood, was one of the unlucky few. He dropped the bus journey and went back to make a second attempt at *darshan*.

Another family could not make it as the family got separated and in the process, they had to abandon the idea and come back to Baltal without *darshan*.

Yet another family, who had the *darshan*, dropped the idea of the rest of the tour with the bus as they were so exhausted that they took a flight back to Faridabad from Jammu.

Many people shared their experiences of the trek and *darshan* with us. A person travelling on his own shard interesting tales of fellow *yatris* in the tent he shared with them. While one was terribly scared of the whole trek and made frantic calls to his family in Kolkata, another obese man, who had to return in the beginning of the trek itself, vowed to Barfani Baba that he would loose weight, become slimmer and fitter and would return for *darshan* the next year. Yet another kept asking him for something to eat, to which this *yatri* confessed that all he had was a packet of glucose, which he was happy to share!

My experience of returning back to Baltal in the night was something I would remember all night. I was curious to know how SK and his group of young boys had fared, trekking on foot, back to Balatal. They had set a target to reach Baltal in flat four hours, but they had not bargained of an unexpected happening. At Burari, a place on the way, SK came across a seventy-years-old woman who sat on the path, in almost a fainting manner. She revealed that her son ran a *bhandara* on the route, a few kilometres away from Baltal and she had somehow got separated from her family.

When SK suggested he get her a horse, she declined, saying she was feeling dizzy and would fall off the horse. On the suggestion that SK arrange for a *palki*, she declined again saying that she would not be steady on that too. So, ultimately, SK and one of his boys supported her from the shoulders and slowly but steadily helped her to return to Baltal, handing her over to her family, a few kilometres from Baltal. In this process they were two hours late and reached Baltal around 11. 30 at night.

SK told me the story of another group of *yatris*. This group, from Bus No 6, had decided to go for *darshan* on foot and hired a *pithoo* to carry their luggage. It was decided that they would meet the hired *pithoowala* at a specified time, at a *bhandara* at Panchtarni.

When the group reached the *bhandara* at Panchtarni at the specified time there was no trace of the *pithoowala*. After waiting for five hours, and contacting the authorities, when there was no trace of him, the group decided to forsake their luggage and proceed to the *gufa* for the *darshan*.

However, a young man from the group had other plans. He worked for an insurance company and all his relevant client data was stored in his mobile, which was in the luggage since his phone did not have connectivity there, it not being a BSNL number.

So, when they came back to Baltal, he decide to once again go to Panchtarini and try tracing the *pithoowala*. Once again he approached the authorities there and the military person, a high ranking official helped him to locate the *pithoowala* in the *bhandara*. The *pithoowala* had been waiting for two days and had stayed put. Having come to Panchtarni for the lost luggage, the young man decided to go to the Cave once again for *darshan*, this time making sure that the *pithoowala* was beside him always. And he had *darshan* of the Barfani Baba for the second time.

The young man once again hired the same *pithoowala* to carry the luggage back to Baltal, from where he moved to Jammu and took a bus back to Faridabad as his bus had already left for Katra.

Understandably the group whose luggage had been lost, were mighty happy to get it back and the young man became a sort of hero for being valiant enough to go back to retrieve the luggage.

Since the Baltal bus parkings are jam packed, it took us nearly half an hour to move out and another half an hour on the road to beat the jam. Then we were set for Sonmarg which is a picturesque town very near to Baltal.

We reached Katra around 12 and had enough time to rest in the guest house which Sunil*ji* had booked for us. Katra was extremely hot and we were sweating on the road. As we stopped at a roadside vendor to have lemon soda, the vendor looked at my daughter's nose and said: *Ye Amaranth ka prasad hai.*

While traveling through Amaranth it is mandatory to take Boroplus with you and keep applying it on the left and right side of the nose as well as on the nose itself to avoid frost bite. The weather was kind to me but my daughter's face was red with the frost bite.

We checked into out rooms. We rested for five minutes or so. Later, after a fresh bath, we dropped dead on the bed for a good three hours.

It was decided that we would move out of the guest house at 4 am. There was enough time to get ready and relax. I took out the suit I had carried for *darsahn* of the Vaishnodevi Mata and got ready. Unlike the *darsahn* of Barfani Baba where we had set forth from Sheshnag without bathing, to avoid delay of *darsahn* due to the bad weather conditions, here I took my time to get ready. We then assembled at the reception of the guest house and set out on foot to the market for a quick meal. The restaurant was a Vaishno *dhaba* and we walked, passing by the colourful and interesting main market of Katra. We had stuffed *tandoori paranthas* with curd. Meal over, it was finally time to head for the *darshan* of Ma Bhagwati.

We reached the auto stand in the Katra market and headed towards the base, the starting point of the trek to the Bhawan.

I had been to Vaishno Devi shrine only once before, with my entire family two years ago. But then, we had gone by helicopter till Sanjhichhat and later taken horses to reach the Bhawan. So this trek was a new route for me.

As we stepped out of the auto, it started raining. We had a wonderful rest and ample time and convenience to dress up, so the rain did not bother us in the least. In fact, it added to the fervor and excitement of the *darshan*. We bought raincoats form the vendors standing nearby and set forth. We had to deposit our purses at security and post security check, and then we were on our way to the trek. We crossed the area for the horse stand, moving ahead.

I wanted to take a horse from this very point, but everyone in the group urged me to walk a little. So I did.

As we walked further, the road was full of people

of all age groups with a good percentage of young kids, brimming with enthusiasm. Both sides of the trek pathway, which is neatly cobbled and even, was lined with shops, either selling grocery items with emphasis on stocking mineral water and beverages along with dry fruits, or little studio shops with a statue of Mata, and a tiger seated in front. People get themselves photographed here to take back memories of the *chadai* and *darshan*.

Since I would get a bit breathless walking uphill, I kept requesting SK to hire a horse for me, but he kept delaying the process, urging me in good humor to walk that extra distance. I reminded him that we had to go back to the guest house and check out of the guest house. So, he finally hired me a horse and I set off trotting while the others in my group went by foot. It was decided that my daughter would meet me at Ardhkumari. Since I had a little doubt about the skills of the horseman, I decided not to give him my sling bag and instead handed it to my daughter.

During the course of the ride, I was pleasantly surprised to see that for most of the distance, there was a separate path for ponies as the road was wide enough. Moreover, unlike the muddy and slippery narrow path of the Amranath Yatra, the cobbled stone road was clean and smooth.

I reached Ardhkumari around 8 pm. I waited for an hour for my daughter but there was no trace of her. And then a fellow member stopped by, telling me that she was taking a short cut. Aghast, I stood there wondering how I would pay the horseman as my sling bag was with her and I did not have a single penny with me. Twenty minutes later SK stopped by. He paid the horseman and asked me to keep the change and proceeded for his *chadai*.

I wanted to take another horse from here till the *gufa*, but I was told I would have to walk several kilometres. I was given the wrong impression that from here one could take an auto till half the distance up to the *gufa*.

I sat down at the café thinking, this time I was not destined to have *darshan* of Mata. For hours, I sat there, watching *yatris* stop for a quick drink and some for dinner. I noticed that the most popular dish was *rajma chawal*.

After a while, the rush in the café began to decline and soon the cleaning man asked the remaining *yatris* to vacate the café. I moved out and sat on the stairs outside. By now, I was beginning to get a little angry at my daughter. How could she desert me, knowing I had no money and could not trek on foot.

I decided, the waiting period was over and it was time for action. My mobile and my wrist watch too were with my daughter. I had removed the wrist watch as it had been raining when we had just started the trek.

I went up to a horse*wala* and requested him to allow me to make a call. He happily handed me his mobile. I realized to my dismay that my daughter used a pre-paid number which was not working here. Her post-paid number was an official one and I could not remember the number as I barely ever needed it, though it was stored in my mobile. And then I finally decided to call my husband in Faridabad. He would make the necessary contacts. But he did not pick up the phone. I had lost all track of time and was astounded when the horseman told me it was 11 in the night.

At that instant I knew I was on my own. The thought of spending the entire night here seemed foolish. Instead, I could slowly walk uphill, have *darshan* of Mata and then decide how to go about things later on.

As I moved further I stopped by at the Shrine Board kiosk and asked the guard seated there, 'How far is the Bhawan from here?'

'5 km.'

'How much time will it take to reach there?'

'Depends.'

'Minimum to maximum?'

'One-and-a-half hour.'

That seemed nothing to me in the face of three hours I had wasted sitting at the café.

'Is that all?'

'Yes.'

And in that instant I decided I would walk one-and-a-half-hour and have *darshan* of Mata. The fact that I had already been here once gave me encouragement to go on my own. So, with a bottle of Pepsi in my hand to take sips at regular intervals to combat breathlessness, I made my way to the top.

The continuous flow of *yatris* on the way kept my spirits high. I also saw several *yatris* sleeping either on benches or on the floor. Here there was no time limit. Everyone trekked at their personal pace. Resting as and when needed. And I finally reached the point from where I could see the Bhawan lights.

It was here that I came across my daughter. I was upset with her, so I simply took my sling bag and moved way without saying much her.

I had managed to walk for 5 km in the middle of the night. The thought of having *darshan* of Mata filled me with tremendous energy. I quickly lined up for the prasad, bought two packets, one for myself and one for Mum, deposited my shoes and sling bag in the locker and moved towards the Bhawan.

It was a great feeling to know that in a matter of a few minutes I would reach my goal, when sitting at the cafe I had almost given up the thought of having *darshan* this time.

The good part was that here, there was not even a second of waiting, as the line in front of me kept moving and my fatigue subsided to the background, my faith making me move. I moved past the security check, deposited the coconut and to the chants of '*Jai mata di*', finally reached the threshold of the *gufa.*

As it was night, the traffic of *yatris* was low, and I took my time walking on the wet red carpet. It was time for the *pindi darshan.* The pandit seated there put a *tilak* on my forehead and guided me nearer to the *pindi* shrine and I bowed my head in reverence.

I walked out from the exit passage and took *chranamrit* from the fountain on the left and kept walking, never taking a break. On the way, I collected my *prasad* of *mishri* which had a coin sealed inside the packet and my coconut.

I passed by the *bhojnaalyaya* and the instant tea dispenser but kept walking as food was the last thing on my mind. As I kept walking, I saw *yatris* sleeping on the floor covered with blankets.

I came to the spot where a sign board pointed to an ancient Shiv cave. Under different circumstances I would have loved to go there, but as I was bone tired I kept walking.

It was around 2.30 in the morning. As I was barefoot, my eyes were on the floor and barely had I crossed the signboard of the Shiv cave, when a creature crossed my path. It took me a few seconds to realize that it was a snake, about 4 inches long, slithering across my path. A feeling of awe overcame me, as this was a symbol of Shiv.

I continued to walk till I reached a STD booth and it was here that I sat down. I shut my eyes, willing my body to relax. And just then I heard a voice, 'Mummy. Here, drink some water.'

My daughter and her friend were beside me. I was grateful for this and drank to my heart's content. It was here that it dawned on me that my Yatra was now complete and it was now simply a matter of returning home.

Since I was tired, we decided it would be best for me to return via *palki*. In spite of the odd hours, we managed to find one. It took me around three and a half hour to descend and by that time it was already daylight. The base camp from where we had started our trek a day before was once again buzzing with *yatris* ready to embark on their trek.

We took an auto for the guest house and it dawned on me that we had been away from home for full nine days.

At 6 pm, everybody had boarded the bus. It was truly the end of the Yatra and beginning of the return journey. It was hard to believe that after an incredible action-packed adventure and *darshan* of both Amaranth and Vaishno Mata, we would be returning to the comfort of home in Faridabad.

During this Yatra, it was not just a test of faith but

also of survival, grit, determination, common sense and a lot more. There were plenty of times when we had to forego basic things and at times compromise on hygiene. But the *sutra* which held us all along was Bhole, and hence we came out as winners.

We stopped at a roadside *dhaba* near Gurdaspur for a break. Here too, there was no toilet, so we had to make use of the bushes.

Uncle, for many stops now, would not get down from the bus. I handed him a packet of biscuits and he took them, sipping Frooti with them.

The night was spent travelling and in the morning we stopped for freshening up at Solakhiyan village on the highway, the same spot we had passed by while going to Amarnath. As we walked towards the bathroom, the sound of Gurbani filled the air. I sat down on the square under the Pipal tree, watching other *yatris* from all the six buses.

This time, unlike while going to Amaranth, there was no frenzy in the bathroom, but a relaxed pace. Majority of the *yatris* preferred not to bathe as home was just a few hours away.

We took off form Solakhiyan and stopped at yet another *dhaba* for breakfast. I ordered stuffed *paranthas* with *lassi*. And my stock of mineral water. It was the last meal we had before reaching home.

Uncle had complained of pain in the abdomen. So it was decided that we would stop at Pipli for providing him some medical assistance. On reaching Pipli, Uncle was treated by a doctor. He was fitted with a catheter and we all felt relieved that he had been treated for his condition.

We crossed Panipat and I realized Delhi was near. An hour and a half later we hit Delhi. From the snow-capped mountains and glaciers, we were once again back to the concrete jungle of the National Capital Region. Traffic on the roads, shops on both sides, street vendors, hoardings of commercial advertisements and politicians greeted us on the way as we headed towards Faridabad via Ashram.

At Ashram, I phoned my husband to meet us at Badhkal. Uncle too called up his family to inform them that he had reached Ashram.

Suddenly the aching muscles and joint pains seemed to subside. At least for a brief time. The physical strain of the past 10 days seemed to disappear at the welcoming thought of home. I had never felt so excited about Badkhal Lake chowk before in my life.

The bus stopped at Badkhal chowk. We picked up our bags and rushed out of the bus, unable to contain our excitement. My husband was already there. We took out the remaining luggage form the bus, paid money back to the members from whom we had borrowed during the course of the Yatra.

A few of my daughter's friends had also got down to help us retrieve our baggage. As I moved towards the car, I spotted Uncle at the bus steps. He looked dazed and was being carried by three men. I was amazed to see him in this condition. It seemed unbelievable that the man who had taken the Amarnath Yatra, year after year for more than a decade, could not get down from the bus.

I quickly called to my husband, asking him to help Uncle into the waiting car. His daughter and son-in-law had come to take him home.

And then I sat in the car and headed home.

As I reached home, I quickly scanned the living room, searching for familiar objects. Everything was in its exact place, Yes, this was home, sweet home.

I dumped my sling bag and rushed to the bedroom and took out fresh clothes and headed to the bathroom. I requested for a glass of cold coffee. For someone whose day begins with a glass of cold coffee, and followed by two more glasses during the day, to have to do without it for a full 10 days was a feat. As the familiar liquid went down my throat, I felt joy and happiness and finally sprawled on the bed.

A few minutes later, I remembered Uncle. I asked my husband to go to his house and enquire about his health. He did that and came back and told me it was just fatigue.

Relived, I slipped into a deep sleep. I got up three hours later. Even though my body was still tired I knew my damp clothes and luggage needed attention.

As I went to unpack, my husband walked in. He looked at me quietly and then said: Uncle is no more.

It took a few seconds for the words to sink in. My mind went to his dazed looks and inability to get down. Never in my wildest imagination could I have expected this fatality. I started crying, questioning Lord Shiv for this unwanted piece of news.

The euphoria of the Yatra vanished in a moment.

I quickly changed into a fresh suit and ran to his house. It was past nine in the night.

Uncle lay on the floor of the living room, covered with a white cloth. The same living room where he had handed me the two forms and card containing the route, the very first day I had gone to his home for guidance.

His son-in law had his arm around his wife, who was sobbing bitterly as she never got to meet him. Two women from my neighborhood came and sat beside me Though it was difficult to talk, I told them about Uncle's failing health towards the last leg of the Yatra.

I stared helplessly at the scenario and finally found the courage to go to meet Auntie. I just held her hands and hugged her. The two neighbours seemed to understand my dilemma and asked me to go home and rest, and telling me that the cremation would be on the next day, at 9 in the morning.

Uncle was cremated the next day. My husband and I placed a shawl over his body as a mark of respect.

The tour operator and his son, who had accompanied us, placed a red *chunni* and flowers on his body.

His body was taken to the Shiv Shakti Mandir, which he loved so much and where he would spent a large part of his day and finally to the crematorium for his last journey on earth.

Uncle's death barely an hour after I returned from Amaranth Yatra, gave a deeper philosophical perspective to my Yatra, and to life.

And this is how my Yatra went.

All That You Must Know

Days later, when back home in Faridabad, we heard about the high number of deaths in the ongoing pilgrimage. The Shri Amarnath Shrine Board officials said that the pilgrims did not come prepared for the arduous journey even though the SASB had carried out a massive awareness campaign about the Dos and Don'ts on the pilgrimage.

It is practically not possible for everyone to visit the Holy Cave due to the difficult conditions like high terrain, unexpected weather, less oxygen, inadequate physical fitness. Each and every *yatri* is required to carry a medical certificate issued by a registered medical practitioner (MRP) that he/she is fit to make the journey.

The Governor of the state has stressed the need for ensuring that all required security related arrangements are firmly in place every year when the annual pilgrimage takes place.He also emphasised the need for day to day coordination among all concerned state government agencies, civil and police departments, Army, central police organizations, the Amarnath Shrine Board and all other concerned agencies.

Besides this, there is deployment of the Mountain Rescue Teams (MRTs) of the state police at identified locations on both the Yatra routes, Joint Control Rooms and Disaster Management Centres and their effective coordination with the meteorological departments, deployment of fire fighting units at identified locations, provisions of adequate number of X-ray baggage scanning units at appropriate locations on both the Yatra routes and installation of CCTV cameras at important locations in the Yatra area.

I now feel compelled to share a few important things with the reader.

Now that you know the details of my experience of the 48 hours leading up to the top for the *darshan* of the ice Shivling and back to Baltal, let me give you a few basic tips for the Yatra.

- Never start the trek on an empty stomach, regardless of whether you are going by foot, by horses or *palki*. It is tiring and you need your energy and nourishment. Carry two or three packets of dry fruits: almonds, cashew nuts, raisins and walnuts. These don't perish, are easy to carry, occupy very little space. The nuts can also be easily stored in your pockets and you keep munching them while trekking. They will keep your body warm in the cold weather and give you instant nourishment and energy.
- Make sure you are either wearing a dress which has safe pockets to carry money, or better still a sling bag which can hold little money. Even if you are going in a group, always carry some money with you. Invariably the group members get separated for short intervals and you will require the money to buy basic stuff like mineral water, a packet of biscuit, *namkeen* or a juice or some similar stuff to get the required energy for the Yatra.
- Also, at high altitude, and low oxygen areas one is likely to suffer nausea. So it is very important to carry sour items like *anar dana*, *imli*, *kairi* sweets, orange sweets, *hing dana*, *lemon churan*

etc in your pockets or sling bag, and keep one in your mouth as you trek forward.

- Once you are approaching Sheshnag and at the *gufa* itself, make sure you have small packets of glucose, which you can eat directly for instant dose of energy and to combat breathlessness.
- Most important tip: Never ever think of going on the Yatra on your own. You must have a companion. Someone close. A loved one, a relative, a close friend, good neighbour.

This is because you never know at which point of the difficult trek you might need care and assistance which only a close companion can give you, despite the medical help available. For me, my daughter filled in whenever I ran into obstacles.

Lastly, the purpose of describing the Yatra experience is not to scare you, but give you a realistic picture of the same. Remember, this is not a holiday. This is a pilgrimage. And the entire stretch from Pahalgam, back to Baltal is the domain of BHOLE. Every short step taken has the *goonj* (the name) of Bhole. And at every juncture Lord Shiv will bless and protect his devotees.

Every year a few *yatris* out of the lakhs that visit, loose their lives while doing the Yatra. This is indeed unfortunate, and the Amarnath Shrine Board tries to do everything not only to prepare the *yatris* for this arduous Yatra, but also provides support at every point of the Yatra, be it in the form of *bhandaras*, low-cost tented accommodation, and above all, expert security and medical care.

The Shrine is managed by Shri Amarnathji Shrine Board (SASB), that was constituted by an Act of the Jammu & Kashmir State Legislature in 2000, with His Excellency, the Governor of Jammu and Kashmir as its ex-officio Chairman. The Amarnathji Shrine Board is responsible for the better management of the Shri Amarnathji Yatra, upgradation of facilities for holy pilgrims and matters connected therewith or incidental thereto. Assisted by a Chief Executive Officer who is a senior IAS officer, and eight distinguished Board Members, the Board is constantly working towards making this journey the a most cherished one.

Role of the Board

The following roles and responsibilities have been assigned to the Shri Amarnathji Shrine Board (SASB) as per section 16 of the Act:

- To arrange for the proper performance of worship at the Holy Shrine.
- To make arrangements for the safe custody of the funds, valuables and jewelry and for the preservation of the Board Fund.

- To undertake developmental activities concerning the areas of the Shrine and its surroundings.
- To make provision for the payment of suitable emoluments to the salaried staff.
- To make suitable arrangements for the imparting of religious instruction and general education to the pilgrims.
- To undertake for the benefit of worshippers and pilgrims:
    - The construction of buildings for their accommodation
    - The construction of sanitary works; and
    - The improvement of means of communication
- To make provision of medical relief for worshippers and pilgrims.
- To do all such things as may be incidental and conducive to the efficient management, maintenance and administration of the Holy Shrine and the Board Fund and for the convenience of the pilgrims.

The Shrine Board has made ambitious plans for effecting improvements in facilities for the pilgrims. These are:

- Barbed wire fencing with searchlights at each camping site.
- Basic amenities like toilets and shelters with benches were provided at intervals of 2-3 kms.

- First aid, eateries, medical facilities at each camping site.
- A helicopter service from the base camps to Panchtarni (about 6 km from the Holy Cave)

The Shrine Board has this informative health directive for *yatris*:

The Holy Cave of Shri Amarnathji is situated at 13,500 feet atop the south Kashmir Himalayas.

The high altitude trek to the Holy Cave involves exposure to extreme cold, low humidity, increased ultra violet radiations and reduced air pressure.

Under these conditions, one of the common risks for the trekkers is the development of acute mountain sickness (AMS).

AMS,which affects the brain and lungs, is known to occur when you ascend to altitudes over 8,000 feet (2500 m). On the icy heights leading to the Holy Cave, you may find yourself being exposed to the following high altitude ailments of varying degrees:

1. Acute Mountain Sickness (AMS)—AMS is the most common form of mountain sickness and may occur after you ascend to altitudes above 2,500 m. It is characterized by breathing problems, headache, loss of appetite, nausea, vomiting, fatigue, weakness, dizziness and difficulty in sleeping.
2. High Altitude Cerebral Oedema (HACO)—

HACO is a severe form of AMS and occurs due to swelling of the brain tissue which may eventually impair the brain. The illness often manifests itself at night and may result in coma/death within hours. Its symptoms include breathing problems, headache, fatigue, visual impairment, bladder dysfunction, bowel dysfunction, disorientation and partial paralysis.

3. High Altitude Pulmonary Oedema (HAPO)—HAPO results in respiratory failure due to accumulation of fluid in the lungs.

HAPO manifests itself at night (typically the second night of climbing in high altitude areas), progresses rapidly and may lead to fatality within hours. Its symptoms include shortness of breath even when resting, persistent dry cough, bright red stained sputum, weakness, fatigue, drowsiness, chest tightness, congestion and increased heart rate.

Younger people are held to be more susceptible to this ailment as, in exuberance, they are inclined to over exert while trekking.

DOs for the *Yatris*:

1. If you suffer from any pre-existing medical condition(s), it is important that you plan your pilgrimage to the Holy Cave only after prior consultation with your doctor.
2. You may be able to avoid high altitude sickness

by giving your body adequate time to acclimatize. It is, therefore, advised that you don't over exert during the first 48 hours of the Yatra area.

3. You are strongly advised to ensure that you do not take any medicine which is not recommended by a qualified physician or doctor. Use of any medicines without proper medical advice can be harmful or fatal in the high altitude conditions.
4. At higher altitudes, dehydration is common and results in headaches. Consumption of lot of fluids, say about 5 litre of water, juice, herbal tea, etc., every day would be advisable.
5. You are advised to eat lot of carbohydrate-rich diet during the pilgrimage. Carbohydrate rich food is considered to be a good guard against acute mountain sickness.
6. It is recommended that portable oxygen may also be carried on the pilgrimage; it is extremely beneficial, particularly for those who face difficulty in breathing.
7. If you suddenly develop AMS symptoms during the trekking, you should immediately descend to a lower altitude, to a place where you feel comfortable.

You may also promptly put yourself on the prescribed medication and take oxygen.

Efforts should also be made to contact the nearest

medical practitioner /medical facility, stationed en route by the Shrine Board, for further medical advice. Your trek should be resumed only on doctor's advice.

8. The mountains must be treated with respect and attempts to 'conquer' mountains or showing off physical fitness must be totally avoided.
9. You are advised to walk at a steady and rhythmic pace preferably in a group, and not alone.

DON'T for the Yatris

1. You are advised to immediately acknowledge AMS symptoms, if and when they arise. Disregard of symptoms of any potential ailment, merely to avoid awkwardness with the fellow trekkers, can be lethal.
2. You are advised to avoid alcohol, caffeinated drinks, smoking, sleeping pills and strong painkillers during the trek and particularly ensure against any such consumption after the appearance of any AMS symptom.
3. The altitude at which your sleep on any night should not be at a place which is 300 m or more than the altitude of the place at which you slept on the previous night.
4. Do not fail to consume sufficient food and fluids. As you may suffer from loss of appetite at high altitudes, you should force yourself, if necessary, to consume adequate nourishment.

The SASB always asks the devotees to immediately contact the nearest medical camps in case of any health issues, to obtain timely medical attention.

Over 32,000 pilgrims were given medical aid in eight camps along Pahalgam and three camps on the Baltal route in the first two weeks of the Yatra 2012.

Once back in Faridabad, I would keep checking newspapers, TV and online for news about the Yatra.

NDTV reported that sixteen Amarnath pilgrims were killed and 16 others injured when a truck carrying them plunged into a deep gorge in Samba district of Jammu and Kashmir . The truck carrying 34 pilgrims, who were engaged in setting up a community kitchen at Amarnath, was returning back when it skidded off the road and rolled down deep into the gorge near Zamoorha Morh in Mansar belt of Samba district, about 50 km from Jammu city.

The Police, Army and BSF had rushed to the spot. Sixteen injured pilgrims were taken to the Government Medical College in Jammu. Nine pilgrims had died on the spot and seven others succumbed to their injuries on the way to the hospital. Two other pilgrims on the vehicle who sustained minor injuries were discharged after first-aid.

This was the second major accident involving Amarnath *yatris* in Jammu region in 2012.

In another incident 15 pilgrims were killed when a SRTC bus bringing them back from the Yatra had rolled down into gorge near Ramban on the Jammu-Srinagar National Highway in July 2012.

So yes, accidents are prone to happen in the Yatra, but the same could happen if you go on any journey to a hill station. So, this piece of information should not be a deterrent to one's resolve and desire to go for Amarnath Yatra.

The increasing number of deaths caught the attention of the Supreme Court of India too.

On 15 July 2012, the Supreme Court took suo-moto cognizance of the deaths of 67 Amarnath pilgrims in the first 17 days of the Yatra. Referring to a clear disregard for human life, the Supreme Court cited the Constitutional rights to life [Article 21] and freedom of movement [Article 19(1) (d)] in India and issued notices to the Central Government, Government of Jammu and Kashmir and the head of the Amarnath Shrine Board. Subsequently, a high-powered committee was constituted to investigate the reasons behind the deaths.

On 31 July 2012, when the Association of Parents of Disappeared Persons (APDP), held its regular monthly meeting where various issues confronting the struggle of the family members of the disappeared were discussed, the recent suo-moto cognizance of the Supreme Court regarding the deaths of Amarnath pilgrims and the governments' continued indifference towards the sufferings of the family members of the disappeared were also raised.

In 2011, 107 people had lost their lives while performing this Yatra. This was the reason why the Shrine Board had made it compulsory that every *yatri* had to be registered and produce a medical fitness certificate by a practising doctor.

Authorities at the camp said thick snow cover at the Amarnath cave shrine route posed multiple risks to pilgrims and has increased the challenges before the organisers of the annual pilgrimage.

Besides the state government, Army and paramilitary forces like CRPF and BSF had also chipped in by setting up a well-knit network of medical camps, which were functional round-the-clock along the two routes and treated thousands of pilgrims.

The SASB had directed all camp directors to use the public address system to urge *yatris* to immediately contact the nearest health camp and take help in case they felt any kind of uneasiness or illness.

The health care facilities were further augmented and over 1000 oxygen cylinders were made available on the two routes to the shrine by the state health department.

"This was in addition to the oxygen cylinders available in the health camps established by the Army, paramilitary forces and NGOs," SASB officials said, adding oxymeters had also been made available at various locations to check oxygen levels of the *yatris* reporting at the health camps.

Additional specialist doctors were deployed at the base camps and at critical places like Brarimarg, Sangam, Pissu Top, Zojibal, Nagakoti to attend to the seriously ill patients.

Various steps had also been taken to improve arrangements for shifting of critical patients to the base camps and, thereafter, to the identified hospitals in Srinagar for prompt and appropriate treatment.

CRPF spokesman Sudhir Kumar said the force had set up various free medical camps including a Cardiac Care Unit and mobile medical camps for saving the lives of *yatris* on both routes. For the first time, a Special Cardiac Care Unit was set up at Baltal.

"Various high-end equipment like nebuliser, laryngoscope, ambu bag, ET tube, CPR mask, defibrillator, patient monitoring system, suction system, advanced oxygen concentrators and emergency drugs were kept available at the Cardiac Care Unit," the spokesman said. over 32,000 pilgrims were given medical aid in the eight camps along Pahalgam track and three camps on Baltal route in the first two weeks of the 2012 Yatra.

Concerned over the rising number of deaths of devotees en route the cave shrine of Amarnath in

2012, a team led by Jammu and Kashmir Health Minister had visited pilgrim camps to review medical facilities provided to them. The team visited camps at Nunwan, Sheshnag, Panchtarni, the Holy Shrine Cave and Baltal. The team also inspected all Medical Aid Centres (MAC), checked the number of doctors and para-medical staff on duty and the availability of medicines, essential diagnostic and treatment equipment and oxygen cylinders.

As many as 83 pilgrims had died in 2012, mostly due to cardiac arrest since the commencement of the Yatra on 25 June, sparking off criticism by Hindu groups who alleged lack of adequate medical facilities.

A spokesman said the high-level team had undertaken the visit on the directions of Governor Vohra, who is also chairman of the SASB, and Chief Minister Omar Abdullah to review medical facilities.

"The team found that the MAC are operating virtually round-the-clock and providing required aid to pilgrims," the spokesman said.

Environment

Besides the death toll of *yatris*, there was another pressing matter to be taken care of: The ecology of the Yatra route.

Amidst concern over polythene bags left by pilgrims along the Amarnath Yatra track, the Jammu and Kashmir Governor had directed that a special sanitation drive be launched to safeguard the ecology of the valley.

"A special sanitation drive should be launched by Pahalgam and Sonmarg development authorities to ensure cleanliness along the tracks and around the camps," Vohra had said, addressing yet another high-level meeting.

The meeting reviewed enforcement of cleanliness and sanitation arrangements which had been put in place in all camps and on both Baltal and Pahalgam routes for the ongoing Yatra.

The Puri Shankaracharya had also expressed grave concern over harm being caused to the ecology of Kashmir by "quintals" of polythene littered by pilgrims along the Amarnath Yatra track.

"Cleanliness is an issue, polythene is going there in quintals every day which is hurting the environment there," he had said after paying obeisance at the 3,880 metre high Holy Cave Shrine. Vohra had reviewed the camp-wise and route-wise sanitation arrangements during the meeting attended by the state Tourism Minister and officers of various departments.

Amarnath Yatra by Helicopter

For those desiring to do the Yatra in a comfortable, stress free way, there is the option of helicopter.

The helicopter services to Amarnath operates from two routes via Baltal and via Pahalgam. Earlier, till 2009, the helicopter used to operate from Baltal to Holy Amarnath Cave but in the Year 2010, the Amarnath Shrine Board relocated the helipad from Holy Cave to Panchtarni. From then onwards, the helicopter operates from Holy Cave to Panchtarni.

Amarnath Yatra by helicopter via Baltal

Baltal is located 15 km north of Sonmarg. The helicopter services operates from Baltal till Panchtarni. From Panchtarni the *yatris* have to trek for 5 km to reach the Holy Amarnath Cave. After *darshan,* the *yatris* have to come back to Baltal to catch the flight from Panchtarni to Baltal.

Advantages of taking helicopter from Baltal

- It is a comparatively shorter route than Pahalgam.
- There are two helicopter companies which operate on the Baltal route.

Disadvantages of taking helicopter from Baltal

There are no hotels in Baltal. The visitors have to stay either in tents at Baltal or in hotels at Sonmarg which is located 15 km from Baltal. There are a few decent hotels in Sonmarg but during Yatra season most of them are full.

Only BSNL connection works in Baltal.

If the *yatris* are not able to come back to Baltal helipad by 5:30pm, they have to spend the night in tents at Baltal because the Baltal-Srinagar highway is closed at night due to security reasons.

Amarnath Yatra by Helicopter via Pahalgam

Pahalgam is located 96 km from Srinagar. This is the most convenient route to reach for the *yatris*, who are planning to go to Amarnath Yatra by helicopter.

Advantages of taking helicopter from Pahalgam

1. As Pahalgam is a famous tourist spot, there are numerous hotels to choose from.
2. Unlike Baltal, all the mobile connections work in Pahalgam

Disadvantages of taking helicopter from Pahalgam

- The package cost is comparatively higher on the Pahalgam route because helicopter tickets are expensive.

General Information

By Air

Kingfisher, Go Airways, Indigo, Jet Airways, Spicejet & Air India operate their flights daily from Delhi to Srinagar. There are direct flights from Jammu, Chandigarh and Mumbai as well.

By Road

Srinagar is well connected to important cities namely Chandigarh (630 km), Delhi (876 km), Jammu (290 km), Leh (434 km), Gulmarg (48 km), Sonamarg (88 km) and Pahalgam (96 km)

By Rail

The nearest railway station to Srinagar is Udhampur, which is about 220 kilometres away from Srinagar. It is well connected to all the cities in India.

The tremendous arrangement made by the Amaranth Shrine Board with assistance from the miitlary and various other government bodies of Jammu and Kashmir state and the abundance of *bhandaras*, by private organizations, have to be seen to be believed

Dr Hansraj Dheer, a doctor by profession and an author by passion, based out of Phagwara in Punjab, aptly titled his book in Hindi on Amarnath as *Shraddha Ka Mahasagar: Shri Amarnath.*

It is only by going to Amarnath that one can experience the outpouring of faith people have for Bholenath, and the insatiable urge to have *darshan* of the ice Shivlingam.

I was fortunate enough to buy a copy of this book from the Nunwan Base Camp.

In the backdrop of the high casualty figure during the 2012 annual Amarnath pilgrimage, Jammu and Kashmir Chief Minister Omar Abdullah had advised people to get "genuine health certificates" which would enable the state authorities to make a correct assessment about their physical ability to undertake the arduous journey.

The Chief Minister was quick to point to "fake" medical certificates being produced by the yatris during the health screening. "On our side, we are trying to put in place a mechanism of health screening but unfortunately, it seems that the health certificates that are being produced are not genuine representations of the true condition of the pilgrim," Omar had told reporters in New Delhi. He had emphasised one needed to see the age profile of the pilgrims who are dying either during this pilgrimage or immediately after it.

"Please understand that these pilgrims have to climb enormous heights in very difficult circumstances, cauring enormous strains on their bodies and particularly on their hearts. Now, with the best will in the world we cannot guarantee everybody's health, particularly if you are going to come with a health certificate that is not a genuine assessment of what your health is," he said.

Appealing to the pilgrims to give right assessment of their health, the CM had said, "we will know whether you should undertake the pilgrimage or not. Cooperate with us..." He had further said, "it is unfortunate that the pilgrims are dying during this pilgrimage...There is a large number of pilgrims this year as compared to previous years."

As the Yatra enterd into its third week, 67 yatris had lost their lives. This was an alraming figure and as expected, it sparked protests from bodis like the Shiv Sena and Vishwa Hindu Parishad.

Shiv Sena protest

Holding the Jammu and Kashmir government and Shri Amarnath Shrine Board responsible for the death of Amarnath pilgrims, the Shiv Sena said, "Shri Amarnath Shrine Board and the state government are responsible for the 62 deaths (of the pilgrims) in a few days after the commencement of the yatra (on June 25)."

Over 1,500 activists of Shiv Sena and Dogra Front took out protest march against the government and the SASB in 2012. The protesters alleged the government and the Board failed to tackle the increasing trend of deaths during the pilgrimage.

VHP accuses Shrine Board

VHP also accused the Shri Amarnath Shrine Board of failing to ensure adequate medical facilities to the pilgrims and demanded a high-level probe into the death of the devotees en route the 3,888-feet high Holy Cave in south Kashmir Himalayas.

"A high level enquiry should be conducted to find out the causes of death so that appropriate steps should be taken to avoid such happenings in future during the Amarnath yatra", the VHP chief had told the media.

Meanwhile, the Shrine Board disclosed that in the case of death of any yatri, the Shrine Board would, at its own expense, shift the dead body from the place of death to the base camp and from there to the Police Control Room at Srinagar for post mortem and other required formalities.

In some cases, the Shrine Board has been providing the required financial support for transporting the dead to their native places.

I hope you will be inspired to go for the Yatra as my narration ends and it has been able to provide you some guideline to prepare you for this Pilgrimage.

I had attended Uncle's Kriya in Hanuman mandir in NIT and now I am writing this chapter of the travelogue.

Uncle's unexpected death just an hour after I reached home gave a philosophical bent to my pilgrimage. For some strange reason I felt that he had to take me to Amaranth and he was alive till I reached home.

He will not be present in person when my book is released but I am sure he will be mighty happy for me, from wherever he is, and will surely accept my gratitude.

Every year lakhs of people visit the Amaranth Shrine. For someone who has not been to Amaranth, they cannot imagine that a whole new world exists there, a world of Lord Shiv.

I started this book with the mantra *Om Namah Shivy*, which means Adoration (namas) to Shiv.

We Hindus believe that a dip in the Holy Ganges in Haridwar rids us of our sins. Sure, nothing wrong in doing that. But going to Haridwar and having a bath in the Ganges is the easiest thing.

A Yatra to Amaranth is by far the toughest in India, and probably in the entire world.

So, why do lakhs of people go to Amarnath each year?

For a diverse range of reasons.

For a once-in-a lifetime pilgrimage.

For the scenic beauty. For the fine weather. To experience snow. For the thrill and adventure. For a unique holiday.

For spirituality.

For the abundance of free *langars* and *bhandaras*.

For the free/low-cost accommodation in tents, to name a few reasons.

Yet, I feel, for many in spite of the powerful glimpse of nature and the strong presence of Lord Shiv in the *goonj* of 'BHOLE', many go back, forget the experience and carry on with their lives.

For me the Amaranth Yatra was an eye opener.

I went there because I have deep faith in God and had recently become a devote of Lord Shiv.

My devotion to Lord Shiv was such that I got a tattoo of Trishul on my body. Not content with that, I commissioned two paintings of Shiv from my art dealer, which now hangs in my living room. And yes, I became a vegeterain too.

This whole thing coincided with the opening of the Amarnath Yatra and I felt a strong urge to go there this year.

Going to Amarnath made me realize the enormity of Lord Shiv, *Devon ka Dev*, *Mahadev* and the symbol of Eternity, beyond birth and death.

It is my personal belief that nature is a creation of God. Nature is a proof and manifestation of the Almighty.

How many times have we seen on TV the devastation caused by a tsunami or an earthquake? But there is a world of a difference between watching this on television and experiencing this in reality. One can only imagine the grandeur of Amarnath Yatra by going there on your own. No amount of video footage or narration can do justice to the reality that is waiting to be experienced.

It is by going to Amaranth that one realizes the insignificance of man before God and the helplessness one feels when one is at the mercy of God – be it in the form of stark terrain and geography, or the extremities and unpredictability of weather conditions.

A pilgrimage to Amaranth should be one of spirituality and not just a mere adventure holiday.

If we can realize the immense power of Lord Shiv, and his boundless compassion for we humans, we will return with a new soul and a renewed perspective on life. For me, the Yatra was more than a dream come true. It was a blessing and realization of Lord Shiv.

Since this trek, even by horses, is very arduous, I suggest anyone who is not completely fit, physically handicapped or old, to go by helicopter followed by *palki*. The *palki* will take you right up to the last seedi, where the Shivling is present.

When Lankapati Ravan prayed to Lord Shiv, he prayed to him in the name of Shankar. The word Shankar is made up of two parts:

Sh + Kar (In Hindi)

Sh means *kalyaan*

Meaning : '*Kalyan Karnewala*'

And since then, Shiv came to be known as Shiv Shankar.

A Pilgrimage to Amarnath should essentially bring a radical change in our lives and should leave us with a bigger vision of life and a new soul.

Here I share two shlokas, translated in English:

If one does good to those who do good, of what merit is one's goodness? It is only the one who does good to even those who do harm to him, is called a saint.

A good person never gives up his nature even when he is caught in calamity. Camphor burning emits more fragrance.

The power and Omniscient nature of Lord Shiv in the universe is felt even by hard core scientists. As I was typing my manuscript, news trickled in that CERN had discovered the "God particle". This appeared more than mere coincident. As I watched the news on TV, I was surprised to know that besides sending a group of top Indian scientists to CERN headquarters, the Government of India had sent a massive statue of Nataraja too.

In his book on Shri Amarnath, Jawahar Dheer has said that Lord Shiv is the harbinger of national unity and '*Chetna*' or realization.

He further says that the *sthapna* of shivlinga in the four directions of our nation has special significance.

In the Himalyas in the North, on one hand we have Kedarnath and on the other Shri Amarnath. Rameshewar in the South, Pashupatinath in the East and Somnath in the West.

Yatris, when travelling to any one of these holy

places of pilgrimage, come in contact with other yatris from all over the nation, they interact with them and experience the richness and diversity of other parts of our great country which helps in establishing national unity, and appreciation and tolerance for different ways of culture and living.

Religion should never be a means to divide us, but a means of appreciation, tolerance and reverence for others. It is amazing that the majority of horsemen at Amarnath are Kashmiri Muslims.

Each religion teaches us about the power and grace of God. Religion should bring together a nation, and the entire world. It should be the binding and bonding factor, becoming a harbinger of world peace, for a better planet.

So, have faith in the Almighty, be a true devotee of Lord Shiv, and he will definitely call you to Amarnath. Experience the divinity of lord Shiv at Amaranth, at least once in a life time, and I promise you, you will be a changed person.

Lastly, I end this travelogue with this shlolka:

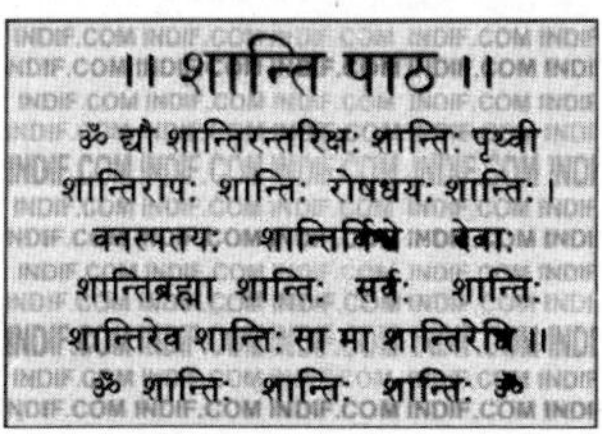

।। शान्ति पाठ ।।

ॐ द्यौ शान्तिरन्तरिक्ष: शान्ति: पृथ्वी
शान्तिराप: शान्ति: रोषधय: शान्ति: ।
वनस्पतय: शान्तिर्विश्वे देवा:
शान्तिब्रह्मा शान्ति: सर्व: शान्ति:
शान्तिरेव शान्ति: सा मा शान्तिरेधि ।।
ॐ शान्ति: शान्ति: शान्ति: ॐ

May there be peace in heaven, may there be peace in the sky; may there be peace on the earth, may there be peace in waters; may there be peace in herbs, may there be peace in vegetations; may there be peace in all the gods, may there be peace in entire Brahma (creation); may there peace everywhere; may there be peace and only peace; may that peace embrace me. OM !! Peace Peace Peace

Jai Bhole!

Finished this draft on 8th July 2012 at 8.35 pm

Sunny's reaction 'Fantastic!!!!!!'

Bibliography

Wikipedia.

Timesofindia.indiatimes.com

English.samaylive.com

Shriamarnathshrine.com

Amarnathyatra2012.in

Ibnlive.com

Sevensisterpost.com

Vedicempire.com

Holyamarnathyatra.com

Telegraphindia.com

Greaterkashmir.com

Kafila.org

A gate erected for the Shobha Yatra at Faridabad

A tableau of Lord shiva at the Shobha Yatra in NIT 2 Faridabad

A line of ponies carrying Pilgrims on the Amarnath trail

All wrapped up in woolens for the yatra.

Pilgrims on Ponies, walking on the ice
with the help of special sticks

The long march
to Amarnath

The treck may be difficult
but it is not impossible

Guarding Faith

Crossing the hurdles

A sign board along the yatra route with the backdrop of snowy mountains.

↑ At Sheshnag, battling the snow

← On the trail at Sheshnag

Standing upright despite the freeze

Pilgrims at midway camps

Shops selling Prasad on the roadside near the Holy Cave

National Flag at Base Camp for Yatra

Desserts at Poshpatri Bhandara

The Kitchen Tent

Helicopter Service at Panchtarni

Restroom Facilities at Camp Sites on the way to Amarnath

The Journey of a Lifetime

Adventure sports at Sonmarg

Rafting at Sonmarg

Sheshnag Lake

At the Door of the Holy Cave

Journey's END

Glossary

Abhishek consecration

Adda gathering

Aloo sabzi potato dish

Aloo tikki mashed potato cutlets

Anar dana, imli, kairi pomegranate seeds, tamarind

Bade chalo, chale chalo get forward

Baksheesh tip

Betaab impatient

Bhajans Hymns

Bhakt Devotee

Bhandaras A shelter offering free food and rest for pilgrims

Bhog The act of offering food to God before distributing to devotees

Bhole ki maya, Kabhi dhoop kabhi chhaya Shiv's magic, sometimes sunshine, sometimes shadow

Chadai trek, a climb

Chana dal sabzi vegetable made of gram/ lentils

Chandan sandalwood

Chappan bhog 56 varieties of food especially prepared as an offering to the Lord

Chutneys sour dips

Daal lentils

Darshan To have holy vision of a deity

Devrani younger sister-in-law

Dhaba a humble roadside restaurant

Dholkis drums and the drummers used in India

Dhoop a type of incense

Dosa a south Indian dish made of fermented rice and lentils

Gajar ka halwa a dessert made of grated carrot and milk

Golgappa a popular Indian snack, a small puri eaten with flavoured water

Goonj echoes

Gufa cave

Gulab jamun a popular Indian sweet made of flour and sugar syrup

Har Har Mahadev Hail Lord Shiva

Hing dana, lemon churan asafodtida and lemon sour powder

Idli a South Indian snack made by steaming rice paste

Jai Bholenath ki Praise of Lord Shiva

Jai mata di Victory to Mother, a popular phrase used in North India for Maa Durga

Jalebis a popular Indian dessert

Jethani elder sister-in-law

Kadai wok-like pan to cook

Karthik a month of the Hindu calendar which falls near the festival of Diwali.

Kheer dona a disposable dish for kheer, an Indian dessert made out of rice and milk

Kurta-pyjamas a trouser-shirt dress usually worn by Indian males during religious occasions

Ladoos an Indian dessert, favourite of Lord Ganpati

Lota a small round utensil, used for carrying water

Makki ki roti an Inian bread made of corn flour, during winters

Mantras Shlokas or religious couplets

Moti choor ke laddoo a popular variety of dessert used during prayer offerings

Mund Mala a garland made out of human heads

Namkeen a salty snack

Palki palanquin

Palki chahiye Want a palanquin

Palkiwalas a person who carried palanquin

Pandal tent

Paneer tikka a snack made of cottage cheese

Paranthas a fried Indian flat bread

Parivar family

Parvaton ke beech main kaisa hai ye Bhola anjaana between the mountains, who is this innocent Shiva?

Patta cloth worn across head during religious occasions

Phirans a warm coat-like shirt worn by people of Kashmir

Pindi darshan Visit to the Holy cave at Vaishno Devi In J and K

Pithoowala a labourer who carried luggage

Poodas a sack made out of gram flour

Poori a fried Indian bread

Prabhaat pheri A group of religious singers who sing hymns early morning during the month of Karthik

Pracheen Shivlaya ancient Shiv Temple

Prasad sacred food distributed to devotees.

Pullian, makhana a form of fluffy rice

Phool makhani a rice snack

Jaap mala an Indian rosary

Chunrie A piece of cloth used to drape over head and bust

Mouli a reddish-colored holy thread tied on hands during religious ceremonies

Rabari a dessert made of milk

Rajma kidney beans

Ras malai an Indian dessert

Samosa an Indian snack with stuffing of potatoes

Sarson ka saag a dish made out of mustard leaves and spinach

Seedhi straight

Sevadhars the religious volunteers

Shagan money offered to someone on a happy occasion

Shaktipeetha the seat of Shakti or the Female diety

Shawls a woollen cloak

Shobha Yatra a religious procession

Tandoori paranthas barbecue Indian breads

Tilak a Holy mark on the forehead, placed by priests in India

Yatra Journey

Ye Amaranth ka prasad hai This is the sacred offering of Amarnath

